Modern Men's Ta...
A Basic Guide To Pattern Drafting

Modern Men's Tailoring
A Basic Guide To Pattern Drafting

Sven Jungclaus
Illustrations by Michael Ross

Bibliografische Information der Deutschen Nationalbibliothek:
Die Deutsche Nationalbibliothek verzeichnet diese Publikation
in der Deutschen Nationalbibliografie; detaillierte bibliografische
Daten sind im Internet über www.dnb.de abrufbar.

© 2020 Sven Jungclaus

Herstellung und Verlag:

BoD – Books on Demand, Norderstedt
ISBN 9783746062310

All rights reserved. It is not permitted to save,
copy or otherwise reproduce this book or any part of it
in any form whatsoever, whether for private or educational use,
without the prior written consent of the copyright holder.

Contents

7	Preface
8	Taking measurements
15	The pants: Step-by-Step Instructions
23	The pants: The pattern
25	Single-breasted vest: Instructions
33	Single-breasted vest: The pattern
35	Double-breasted vest: Instructions
37	Double-breasted vest: The pattern
39	Shirt: Instructions
45	Shirt: The pattern
46	Sleeve for a shirt: Instructions
49	Sleeve for a shirt: The pattern
50	Collar for a shirt: Instructions
55	Collar for a shirt: The pattern
57	Single-breasted jacket: Instructions
66	Single-breasted jacket: The pattern
70	Sleeve for a jacket: Instructions
75	Sleeve for a jacket: The pattern
76	Collar for the single-breasted jacket: Instructions
77	Collar for the single-breasted jacket: The pattern
79	Double-breasted jacket: Instructions
81	Double-breasted jacket: The pattern
82	Collar for the double-breasted jacket: Instructions
83	Collar for the double-breasted jacket: The pattern
85	Single-breasted coat: Instructions
95	Single-breasted coat: The pattern
97	Double-breasted coat: Instructions
99	Double-breasted coat: The pattern
100	Tie, bow tie, plastron: The patterns
101	How to tie a tie and a bow tie
102	Etiquette: what to wear?
104	Washing and care symbols
107	Abbreviations
108	Biography

A few words to start ...

Bespoke

In the age of global mass production, this word unfolds its charm again. While there seems to be tailor-made solutions for everything today, in the 18th and 19th centuries there was no alternative to custom work. Before industrial production, clothing was always individually adapted and later turned into a luxury item - as a counterpoint to commoditized attire.

Bespoke instead of for masses

In the meantime, craftsmanship is appreciated again. Handmade clothes receives new attention and is often the favorite piece. But without an optimal cut, the best tailoring does not work as desired. Patterns are the DNA of a garment, a kind of architecture for textile ideas. The final fit is a successful mix of subtle observation, precise measurement and skillful implementation in an individualized pattern.

Assistance by the pro

In this book, practical step-by-step instructions ensure that inexperienced cutters can work out the perfect fit for suits, coats, pants and more - based on individual body measurements. Over the years cutter and master tailor Sven Jungclaus has refined his know-how in a practical way and is now passing on his knowledge in form of this book in a comprehensible way.

Have fun creating your own pattern!

Why it is important taking measurements the right way.

Just using a measuring tape is not enough. The perfect fit of a garment depends on several factors: on one hand, on the skills of the tailor. On the other hand, on the know-how of the cutter who incorporates his experience in the pattern and at the same time takes into account the characteristics of the respective material. First and foremost, however, correct and conscientious measures are important. This is not just about the numbers determined by tape measure, but much about what a cutter sees. The experienced consideration of the respective stature and posture are basic ingredients for the perfect cut.

Taking measurements already begin with the unobtrusive analysis of the body and the individual posture when a customer enters the tailor shop. As soon as someone knows that he will be measured, he automatically turns himself straight. This artificial posture falsifies the end result, and the awakening ensues at the first fitting when the balance of the garment does not match to the customer.

An old saying among professionals is: "Have three masters measure one person and you will get three different results." This joke can quickly turn into reality if one does not work accurately and conscientiously. The instructions on the following pages will help you to avoid unpleasant surprises.

There are a few tricks to distract the customer and at the same time to determine optimal measurements: It is important not to measure in front of a mirror, this only unnecessarily awakens the vanity. In addition, there is nothing to see before the first fitting anyway. It helps to engage the customer into a conversation and thus distract him. The tailor, on the other hand, should, of course, focus on taking the measurements, despite the small talk.

Instructions for taking measurements

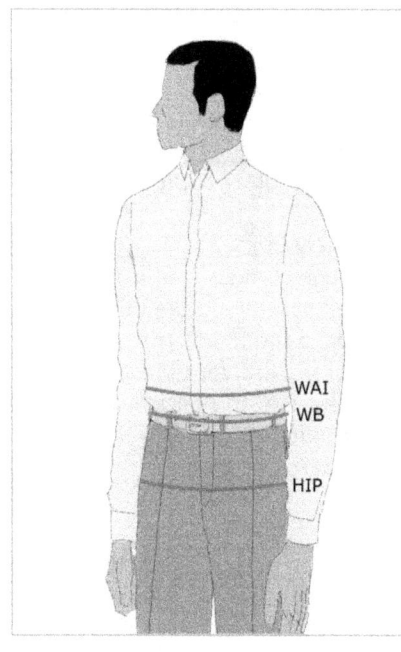

Waistline (*WAI*)
The waistline is measured exactly around the waist, at the narrowest point just above the hipbone. Here a waist measuring tape is fixed.

Waistband (*WB*)
The waistband is measured at the height of the desired position, exactly where the waistband of the pants should sit.

HIP
The hip width, or seat, is measured horizontally around the strongest point of the buttocks.

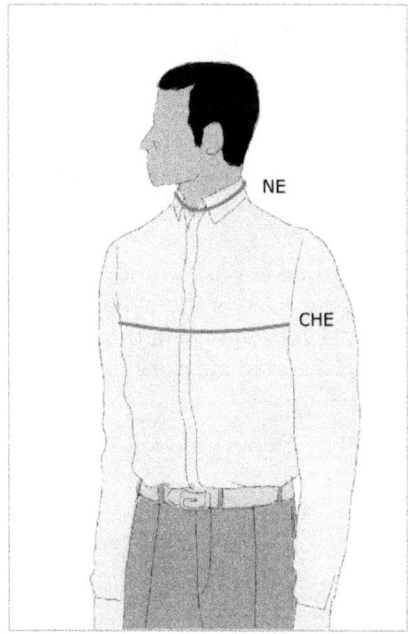

Neck (*NE*)
When measuring the neck, care must be taken that the tape measure is not set too high. The circumference is measured at the base of the neck (on the skin), directly above the collarbone. It helps to keep two fingers between tape measure and neck so as not to measure too narrow.

Chest (*CHE*)
When measuring the chest, the tape measure will be placed around the strongest chest point, then passed under the arms and slightly higher at the back.

Manual for taking measurements

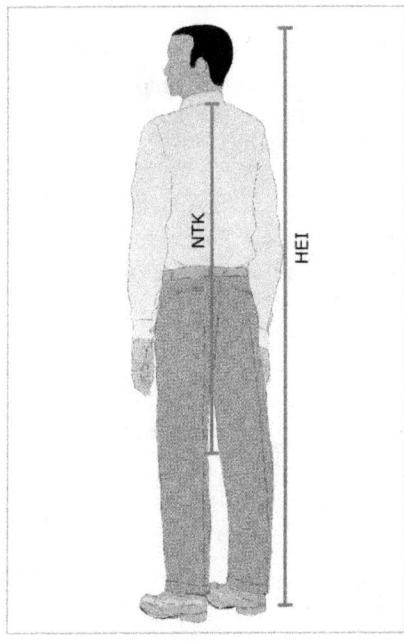

Height (*HEI*)
Mostly, the customer knows his height. If you do not trust this information, it is measured from the top of the head to the sole of the foot, preferably without shoes. Otherwise, simply subtract the heel height.

Nape to knee (*NTK*)
The nape-to-knee is measured from the 7th cervical vertebra along the mid-back across the seat to the knee. The 7th cervical vertebra is the vertebra protruding slightly at the back of the neck - in the pattern constructions it is called the cervical-vertebra-point *CVP*.

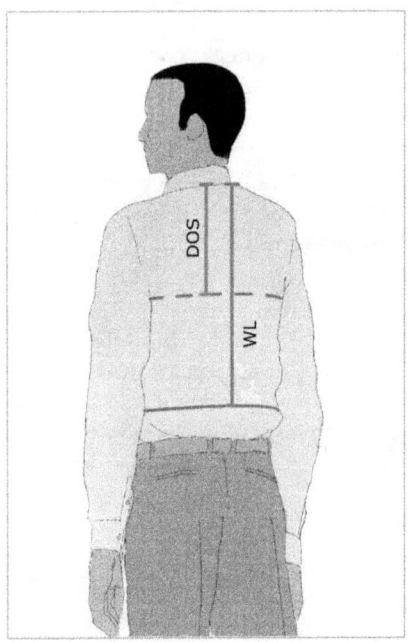

Depth of Scye / Depth of armhole (*DOS*)
To measure the depth of scye, push a piece of cardboard under the customer's arm and measure from the 7th cervical vertebra along the middle of the back to the upper edge of the cardboard.

Nape to waistline / Waist length (*WL*)
The length of the waist is measured from the 7th cervical vertebra along the middle of the back to the tape measure fixed at the waist.

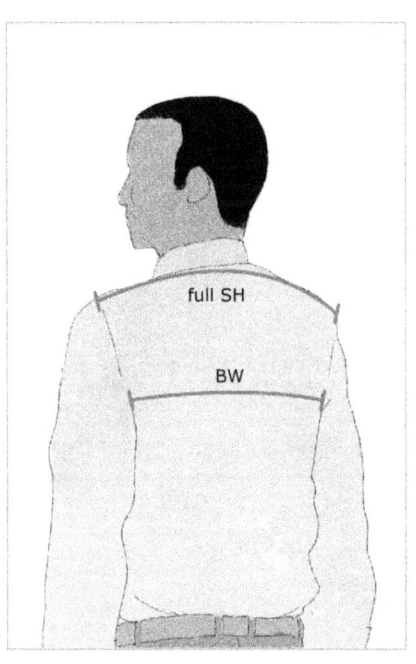

Full shoulder width (*FUSH*)
The entire shoulder width is measured from the left shoulder bone, across the back to the right shoulder bone.

Back width (*BW*)
It is measured across the back in a relaxed position, from the left to the right arm.

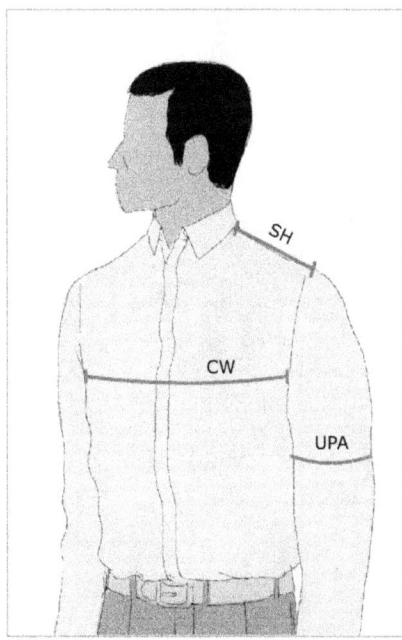

Shoulder width (*SH*)
The shoulder width is measured from the neckline to the shoulder bone.

Chest width (*CW*)
The chest width is measured across the strongest breast point from the left to the right arm.

Upper arm (*UPA*)
For strong biceps, this measure should be read necessarily. It is measured around the strongest point of the upper arm.

Manual for taking measurements

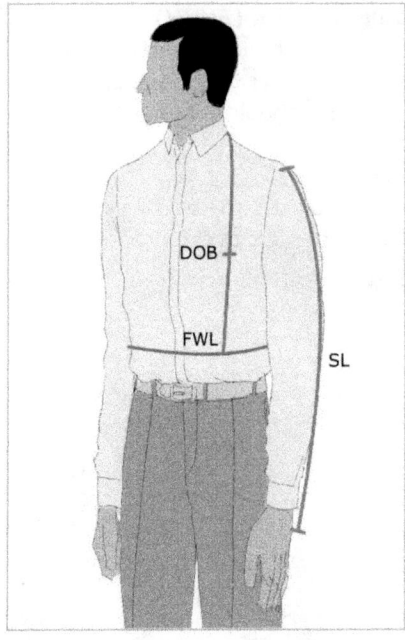

Sleeve length (*SL*)
Measure the sleeve length from the shoulder bone over a slightly bent elbow to about 2 cm above the first thumb joint.

Depth of brest (*DOB*)
The depth of the chest is measured from the 7th cervical vertebra (see explanation *NTK*, p. 10) over the shoulder to the front, to the point of the breast.

Nape to front waist / Front waist length (*FWL*)
The front-waist-length is measured from the 7th cervical vertebra over the shoulder across the breast point, to the tape measure fixed at the waist.

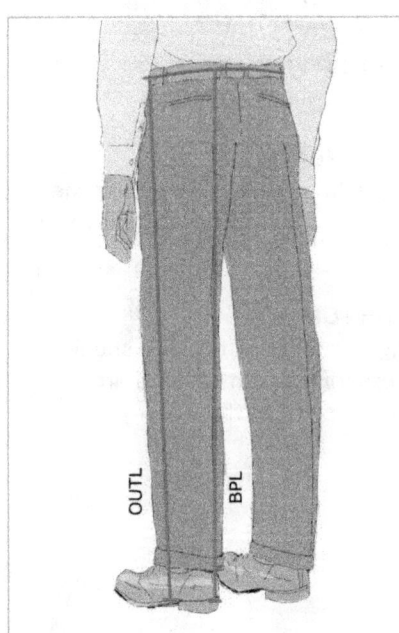

Back pants length (*BPL*)
First, fix the tape measure at the point where the waistband should sit. Now the back pants length is measured from the waistband to the floor.
(If the customer is wearing shoes, measure to the top of the heel.)

Outside leg (*OUTL*)
First, fix the tape measure at the point where the waistband should sit.
Now the outside leg can be measured on the side from the waistband down to the floor.
(If the customer is wearing shoes, measure to the top of the heel.)

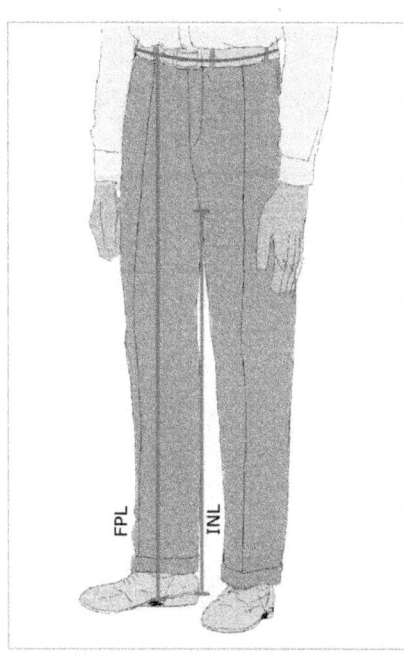

inside leg (*INL*)

To measure the inside leg, have the customer pull up the pants into the crotch. Then it is easy to determine the measurement on the inside of the leg from the crotch to the floor. (If the customer wears shoes, the heel height is subtracted.)

Front pants length (*FPL*)

First, fix a tape measure at the point where the waistband should sit. Now the front length of the pants is measured from the waistband down to the floor. (If the customer wears shoes, the heel height is subtracted.)

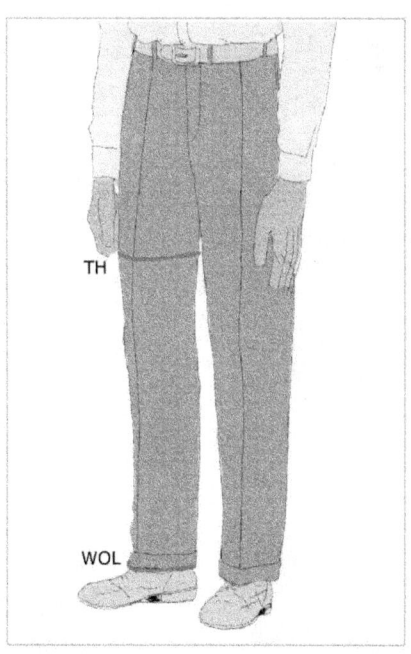

Thigh (*TH*)

The thigh circumference is measured around the strongest point of the thigh, about 10 cm below the crotch.

Width of length (*WOL*)

The hem circumference is measured at the bottom of the trouser hem according to customer requirements.

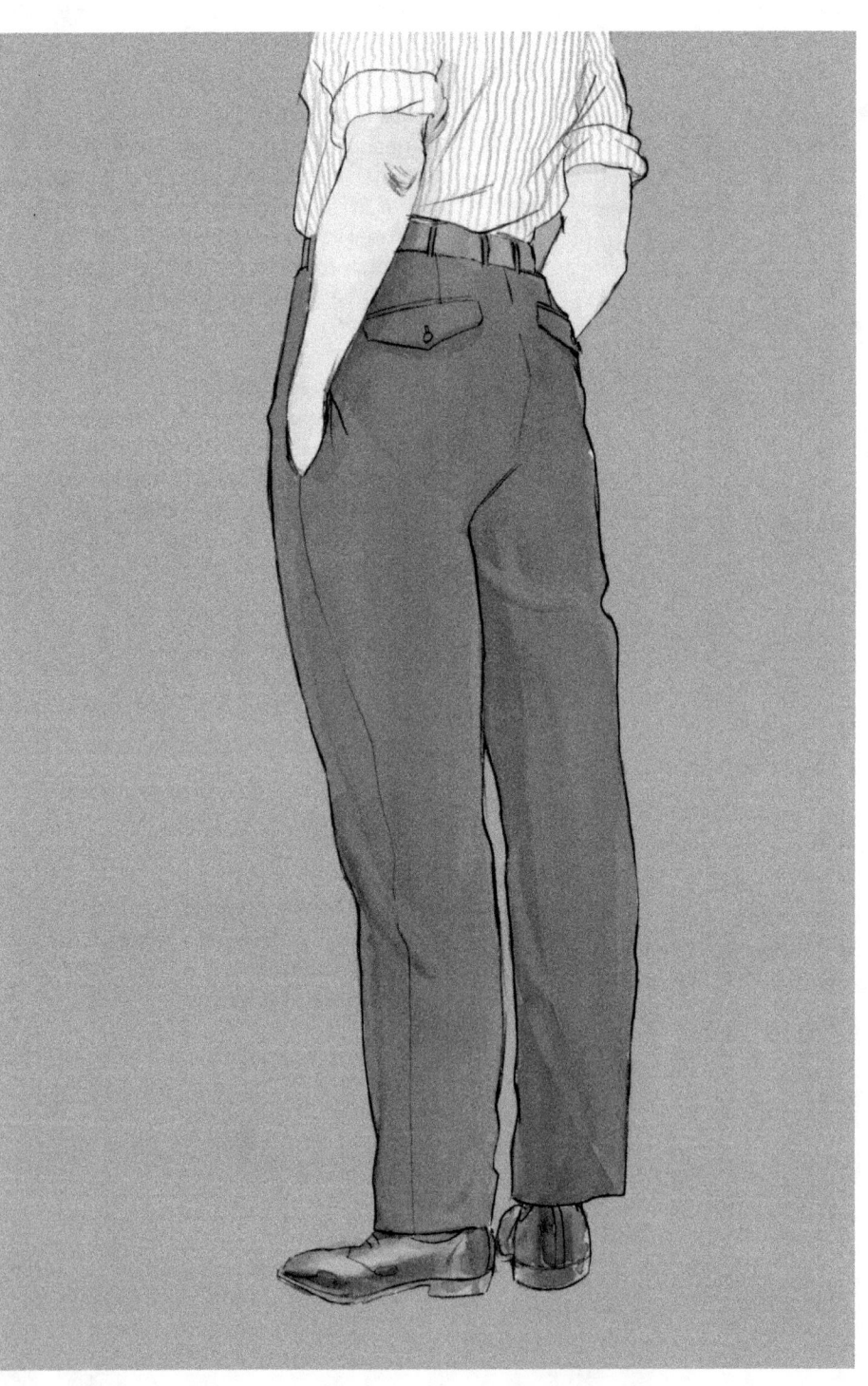

Manual for the pants

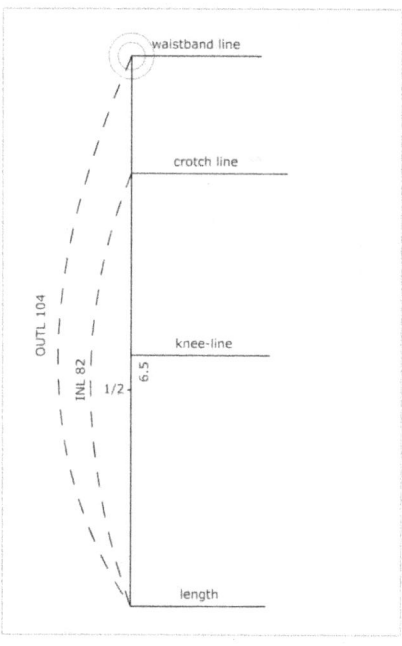

Start basic structure of front pattern
- draw a right angle
- the horizontal line is the waist-line
- from starting point: mark down outside-leg *OUTL* 104 cm and square right, this line is the length *LG*
- from *LG*: mark up inside-leg *INL* 82 cm and square right, this line is the crotch-line
- from *LG*: mark up 1/2 *INL* + 6.5 cm and square right, this line is the knee-line

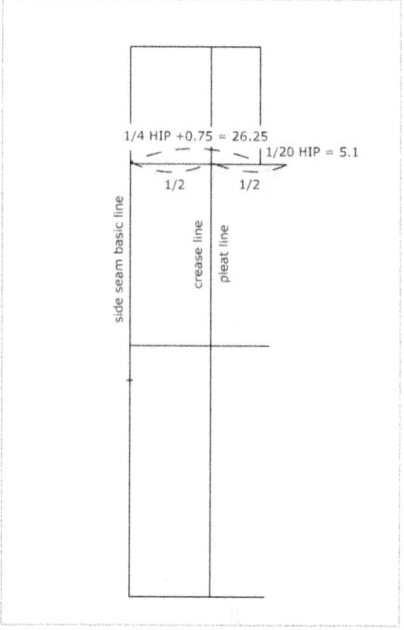

Basic structure
- on crotch-line: from side-seam-basic-line mark to the right 1/4 hip-width *HIP* 25.5 + 0.75 (1/4 depth of pleat at crease) = 26.25 cm and square up
- from this point: mark to the right 1/20 *HIP* = 5.1 cm
- on crotch-line: halve the hole section and square up and down, this line is the crease-line or pleat-line (see also page 23)

With or without pleat
- you will find more informations about the depth of the pleat on page 16, picture 2
- if you draw the pants without pleats, the measurement 1/4 *HIP* will be enough

15

The pants

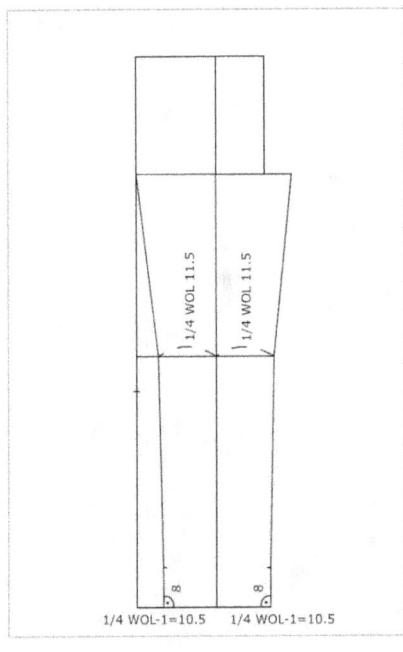

Width of length WOL
- on *LG*-line from crease-line: mark to each side, 1/4 *WOL* - 1 = 10.5 cm, square up and mark 8 cm

Knee-width KN
- on knee-line from crease-line: mark to each side 1/4 *WOL* 11.5 cm
- connect the points at the knee-line with the points on the length
- connect the points at the knee-line with the points on the crotch-line

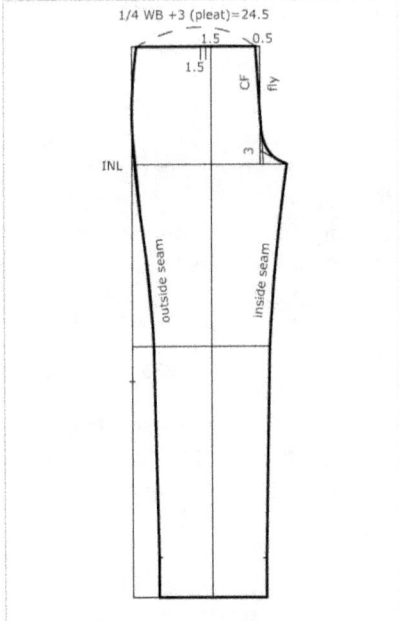

The fly CF
- on the fly-line from crotch-line: mark up 3 cm
- at the front of the waistband-line: mark to the left approx. 0.5 cm and connect with lower point at center-front *CF*
- shape fly seam

The crease
- on waistband-line from crease-line: mark to the left 3 cm (pleat) and square down
- on waistband-line from *CF*: mark to the left 1/2 *WB* + 3 cm (for the pleat) = 24.5 cm

Finish the front-pattern
- shape both, outside-seam and inside-seam nicely
- compare the taken measurements of the front length with the pattern

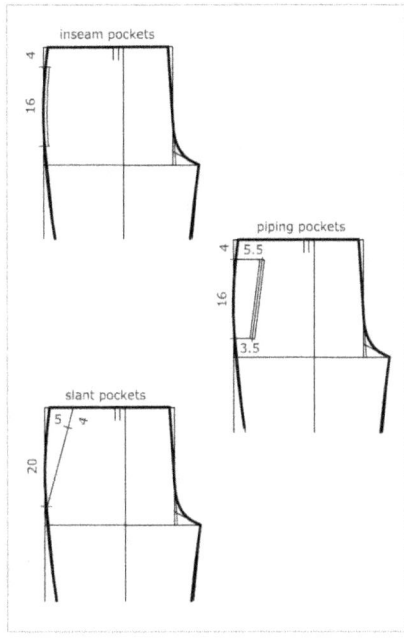

Inseam pockets
- on sideseam from waistband-line: mark down 4 cm
- from here mark down the pocket opening with 16 cm

Piping pockets
- from waistband-line mark down 4 cm, then square right and mark 5.5 cm
- for the lower point of the pockets: mark down length of the pocket opening with 16 cm, then square right and mark 3.5 cm
- connect both points

Slant pockets
- on the waistband-line from side seam: mark to the right 5 cm
- on the side seam mark down 20 cm
- connect both points and from the waistband-line mark down 4 cm

Back pattern
Cut out the front pattern and use it as a basis. Place it on a new piece of pattern paper.

- extend all lines (waistband-line, knee-line, length and crease-line)
- on *LG*-line from front pattern: mark 2 cm to each side, square up and mark 8 cm
- on knee-line from front pattern: mark 2 cm to each side
- connect the points at the knee-line with the lower points

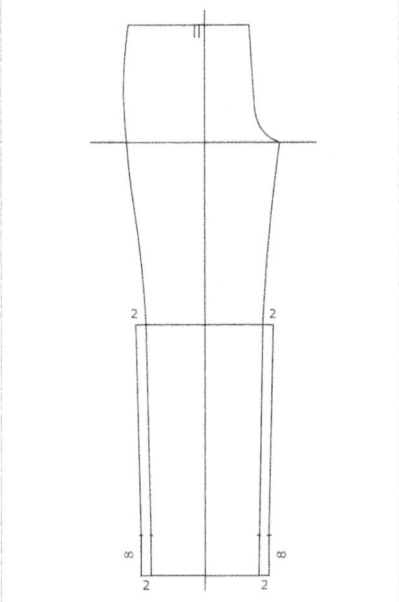

17

The pants

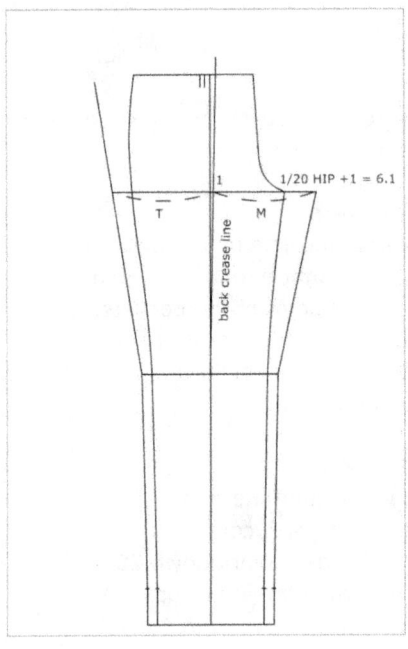

Width of back pants
- on the crotch-line from front-center-line: mark to the right approx. 1 cm
- at the crossing of the front-crease-line and knee-line: draw up a line through the previous point
- this line is the displaced back-crease-line

- on the crotch-line from the tip of the front trousers:
  mark to the right 1/20 HIP + 1 = 6.1 cm

- on crotch-line: measure M the entire distance from the tip of the back trousers to the back-crease-line and transfer T to the left

- finish inside-seam and the side-seam as shown

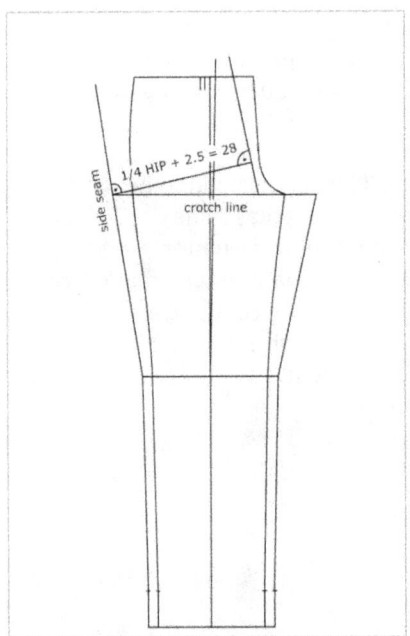

The inclination of the butt seam
- at the crossing of the crotch-line and the sides eam of the back pants: draw a right angle from the side seam to the right

- on that line from side seam: mark to the right 1/4 HIP + 2.5 fullness = 28 cm and draw up right angle

- pierce this point with the tip of the pencil to transfer it to the lower paper

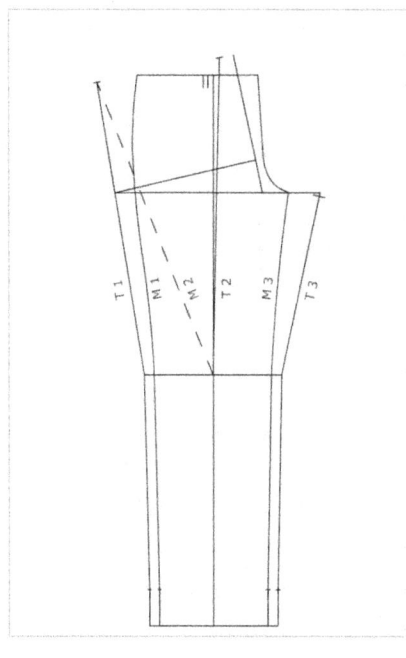

Height of waistband at the back pants
- measure the length of the side seam at the front pants from the knee point upwards *M1* and transfer it to the back pants *T1*

- from the crossing front-crease-line / knee-line: measure up to the side seam of the back pants *M2* and transfer it to the back-crease-line *T2*

- measure here from the top to the length and compare this measure with the taken measurement

- measure the length of the inside-seam of the front pants from the knee-point upwards *M3* and transfer it to the back pants *T3*

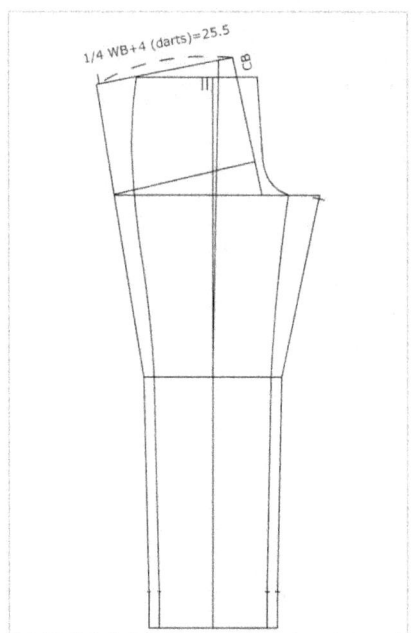

Width of waistband at back trousers
- connect the top points for the waistband of the back pants
- from the center back *CB*:
  mark to the left 1/4 *WB* + 4 cm for darts = 25.5 cm
- this measure should not go beyond the sides eam, otherwise decrease the darts
- for a flat butt, you can do the back pants without a second dart
- if only one dart is required due to a smaller difference between the waistband and the hip, then the fullness at the back-waistband is calculated just with one dart

- remove the front pants and retrace all lines below
- shape inside-leg and outside-leg

The pants

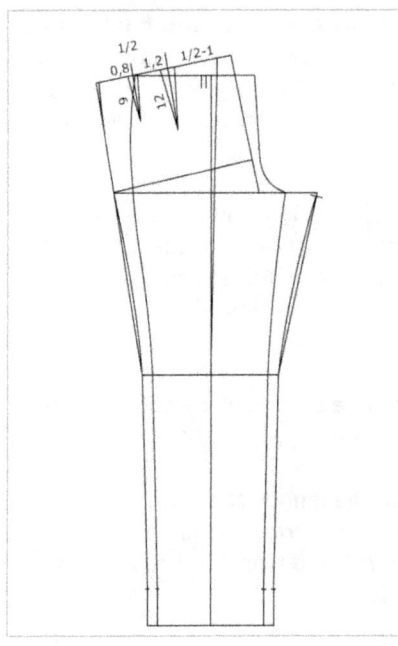

Darts back pants
1. Dart
- at waistband from *CB*: mark forward 1/2 – 1 cm of the entire length of the back-waistband (including fullness for darts) and draw down right angle
- dart length is approx. 12 cm
- the depth of the dart is about 1.2 cm on both sides (it depends on the difference between waistband and hips)

2. Dart
(the number of darts depends on the difference between waistband and hips)
- halve the distance between side seam and 1st dart and draw down right angle
- dart length is approx. 9 cm
- the depth of the dart is about 0.8 cm
- the depth for both darts is approx. 4 cm in total

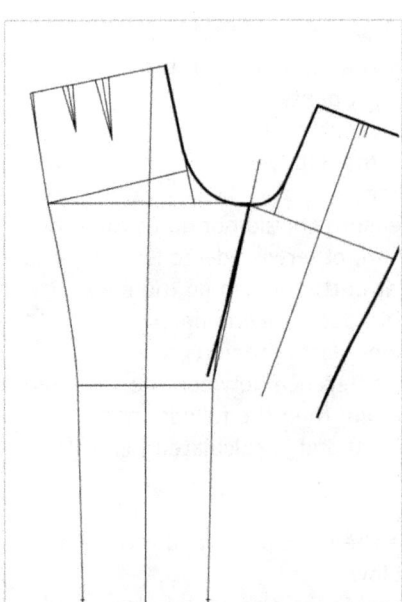

Shaping the seat-seam
- put on the inside-seam of the front pants to the inside-seam of the back pants and shape the seat-seam

Note
Make sure that the arch of the seat-seam is not too flat and definitely not too wide. Otherwise, the back pants will be to tight at the butt.

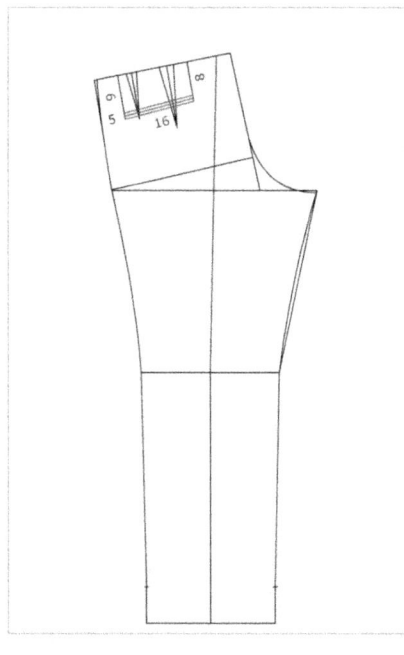

Back-pocket
- from side seam: mark to the right 5 cm
- from waistband at side seam:
  mark down 9 cm
- from waistband at seat seam:
  mark down 8 cm
- draw line for the back-pocket and mark approx. 16 cm for the opening

Fullness
At the waistband, the measure should be exactly right. The fullness at the 1/2 hips should be about 2.5 cm if you draw without pleats and about 2.5 cm + 1/4 of the pleats-measure if you like them with pleats. (1/2 *HIP* + 2.5 cm fullness or 1/2 *HIP* + 2.5 cm + 1/4 of the pleats)

Cutting
- cut front pants 2 x
- cut back pants 2 x

Instructions
- all measures are in cm
- all seams are without seam allowances
- the lower parts of the crease-line of the front and back pants serve as the grainline

Measurements for the pants

	1/2	1/4
Waistband (*WB*)	86	43	21.5
Hips (*HIP*)	102	51	25.5
Outside leg (*OUTL*)	104		
Inside leg (*INL*)	82		
Width of leg hem (*WOL*)	46	23	11.5

Seam allowances

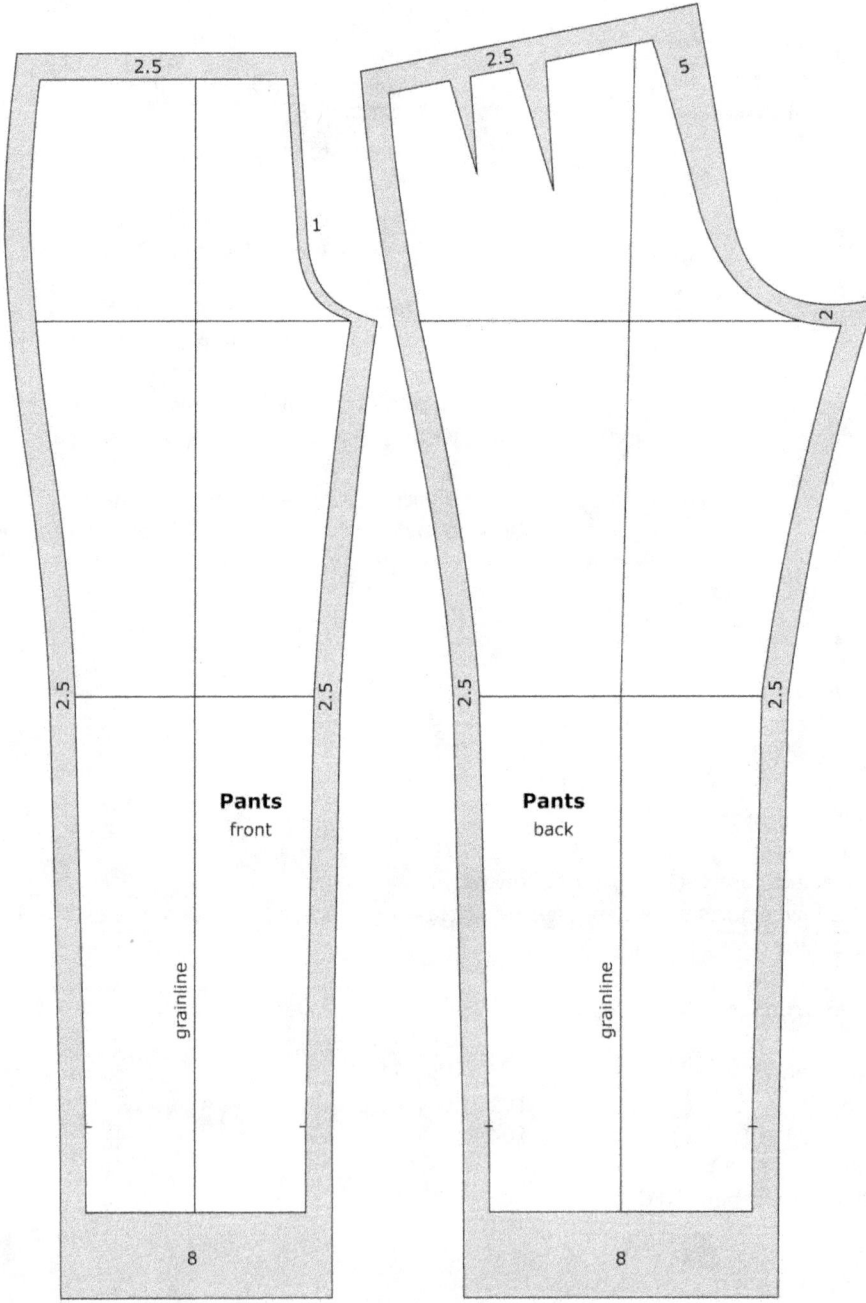

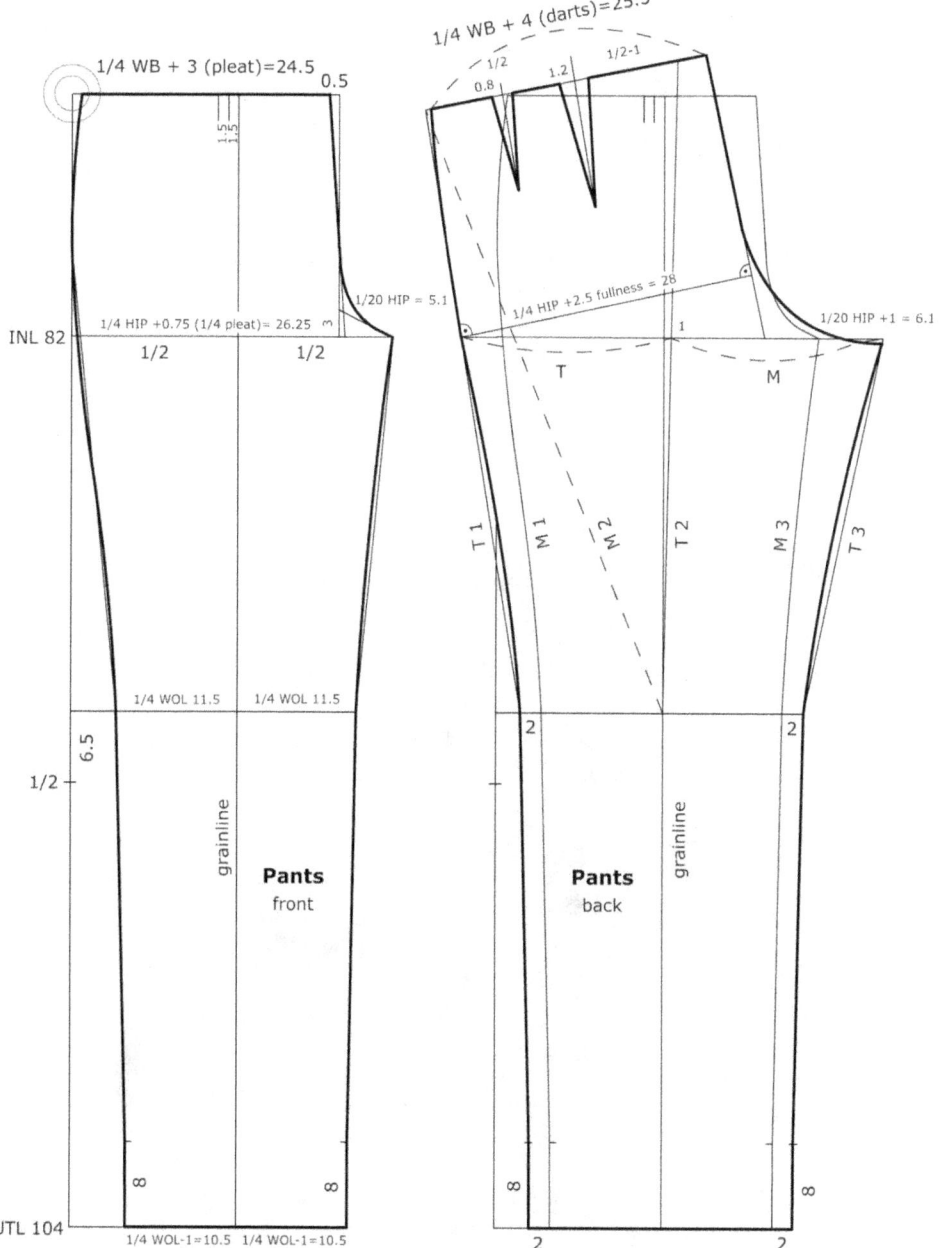

Manual for a single-breasted vest

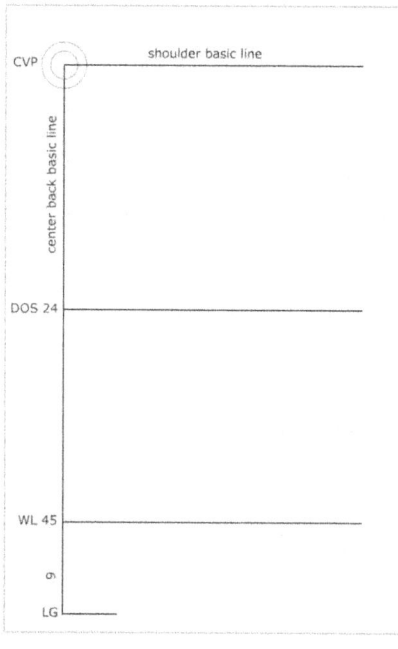

Start
- draw right angle
- vertical line is the center-back-basic-line
- horizontal line is the shoulder-basic-line

- on center-back-basic-line from 7th cervical-vertebra-point CVP: mark down depth-of-scye DOS = 1/16 HEI + 1/8 CHE = 24 cm and square right
- on center-back-basic-line from CVP: mark down waist-length WL = 1/4 HEI = 45 cm and square right
- on center-back-basic-line from WL: mark down 9 cm and square right

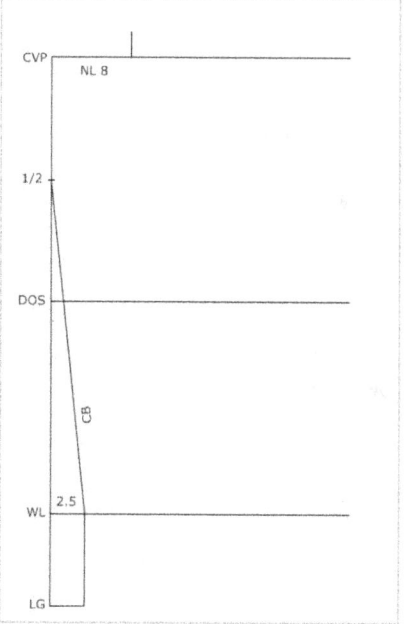

Center-Back-Seam
- on center-back-basic-line: halve the line between CVP and WL
- on WL-line from center-back-basic-line: mark to the right 2.5 cm and square down
- connect this point with previous point
- This line will become the center-back CB

Neckline, Shoulder
- on shoulder-basic-line from CVP: mark to the right neckline NL = 1/6 NE + 1 = 8 cm and square up

25

The single-breasted vest

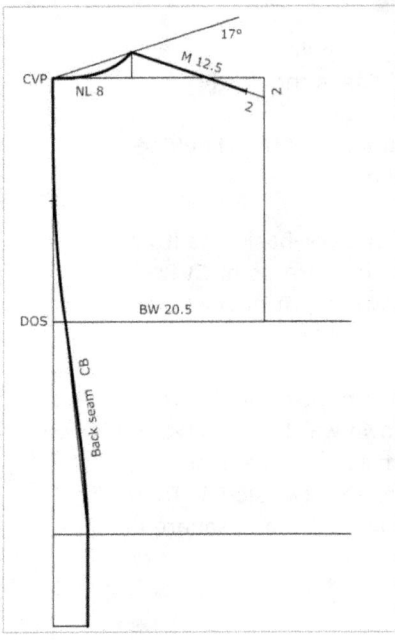

Center-Back-Seam
- shape seam at center-back CB

Shoulder
- on chest-line from seam at CB: mark to the right back-width BW = 2/10 CHE = 20.5 cm and square up

- from CVP create 17° angle to the right up
- on BW-line from shoulder-basic-line: mark down 2 cm and connect this point with previous point at neckline
- mark shoulder seam from BW-line 2 cm narrower and measure this line M = approx. 12.5 cm (you will need this for the front shoulder)
- shape back-neckline

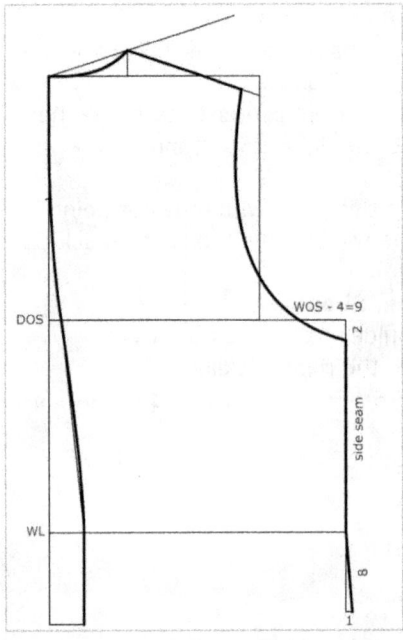

Sideseam
- on chest-line from BW-line: mark to the right width-of-scye WOS - 4 = 9 cm and square down
- at sideseam from chest-line: mark down 8 cm, square right and mark 1 cm on this line to widen this part for the hips
- shape side seam nicely

Armhole
- at side seam from chest-line: mark down 2 cm
- shape back armhole nicely
- this armhole enlargement is to give the wearer more room for moving his arms

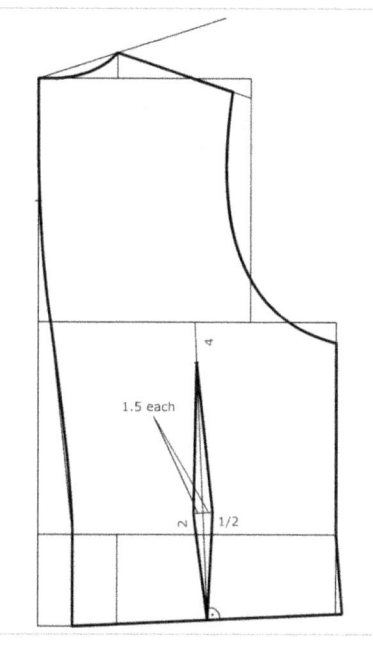

Hem
- connect lower point of *CB* with lower point at sidecseam

Dart
- at the back: halve *WL*-line
- from hem: draw up right angle through previous point
- from chest-line: mark down 4 cm
- from *WL*-line: mark up 2 cm and draw right angle
- mark depth of the dart with 1.5 cm each
- finish dart as shown
- the depth of the dart depends on the difference between *CHE* and *WAI*, so this can also be less or more (up to 2.5 cm)

Grainline
- the center of the dart serves as the grainline

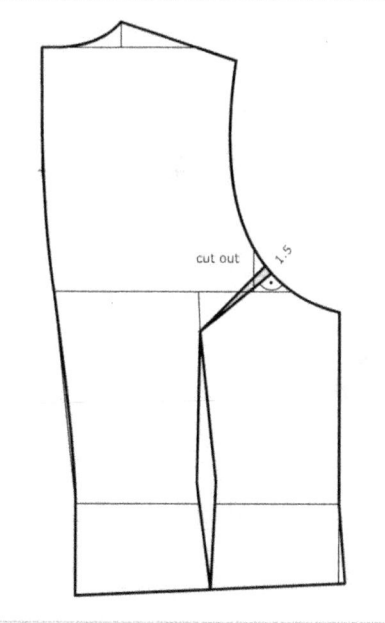

Narrow armhole
- from armhole: draw right angle toward the dart
- mark about 1 to 1.5 cm to cut out
- cut out this amount and join together.
- this opens the back-dart and the back gets a better fit at the armhole and around the scapula
- the shape of the armhole should be well-balanced after joining together (see also pattern on page 32)

The single-breasted vest

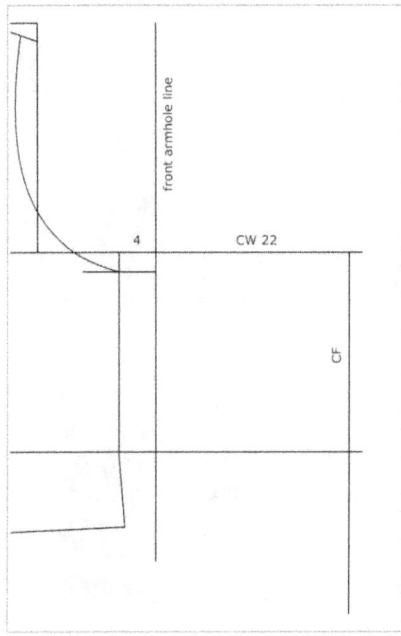

Basic front frame
- extend chest-line and *WL*-line

- on chest-line from side seam: mark to the right 4 cm (this is the amount subtracted from the width-of-scye *WOS* at the back armhole) and square up and down
- this is the front-armhole-line
- from here on chest-line: mark to the right chest-width *CW* = 2/10 *CHE* + 1.5 = 22 cm and square down
- this line is the center-front *CF*

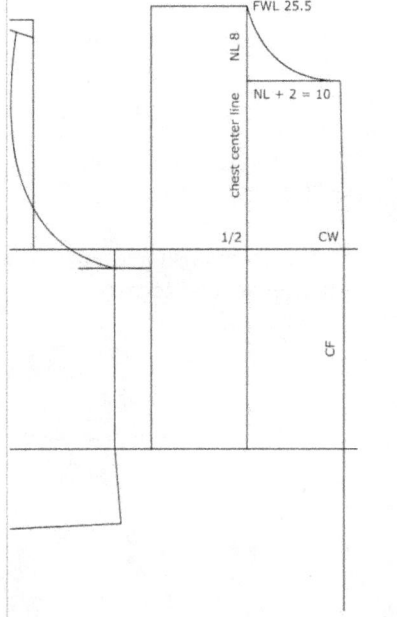

Neckline
- halve chest-width *CW* and square up and down
- this is the chest-center-line or front-dart-line
- on this line from chest-line: mark up front-waist-length *FWL* = *DOS* + 1.5 = 25.5 cm and square left
- this is the shoulder-basic-line
- on chest-center-line from shoulder-basic-line: mark down front neckline *NL* = 1/6 *NE* + 1 = 8 cm square right and mark *NL* + 2 = 10 cm
- connect this point with *CF* on chest-line
- shape neckline

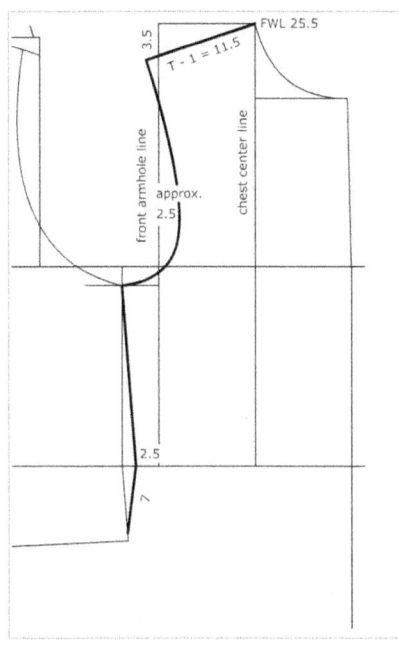

Shoulder
- at front-armhole-line from shoulder-basic-line: mark down 3.5 cm
- connect this point with point at neckline and transfer *T* measure from back-shoulder - 1 cm = 11.5 cm

Armhole
- shape front armhole nicely

Side seam
- at *WL*-line from front-armhole-line: mark to the left 2.5 cm
- from this point draw down 7 cm so that the line touches the back sideseam
- connect point at *WL*-line with front armhole
- the side seam at the front-part sould be 1 cm shorter than at the back part

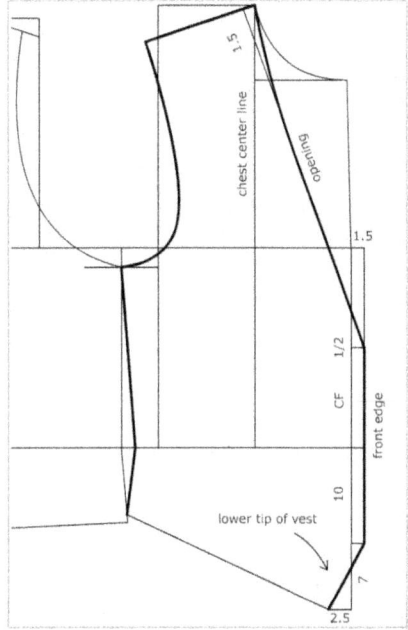

Opening
- at shoulder tip: mark to the left 1.5 cm
- at *CF* between chest-line and *WL*-line: halve the distance, square right, mark 1.5 cm and square down
- connect point at front edge with upper neckline
- shape opening by hollowing it slightly

Tip of vest
- at *CF* from *WL*-line: mark down 10 cm and square right
- from this point: mark down 7 cm, square left and mark 2.5 cm
- connect this point with marking at front side seam
- finish tip of vest at lower front edge

The single-breasted vest

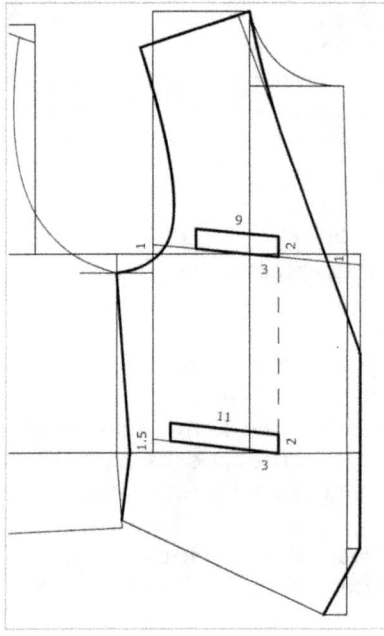

Top pockets
- at front-armhole-line: mark up 1 cm
- at front edge from chest-line: mark down 1 cm
- connect both points
- from chest-center-line: mark to the right 3 cm and square down parallel to the CF
- mark width of bar (welt-pocket) with approx. 2 cm
- mark pocket-opening with approx. 9 cm

Lower pockets
- at front-armhole-line from WL-line: mark up 1.5 cm
- on WL-line from chest-center-line: mark to the right 3 cm and square up
- connect both points
- mark width of bar with approx. 2 cm
- mark pocket-opening with approx. 11 cm

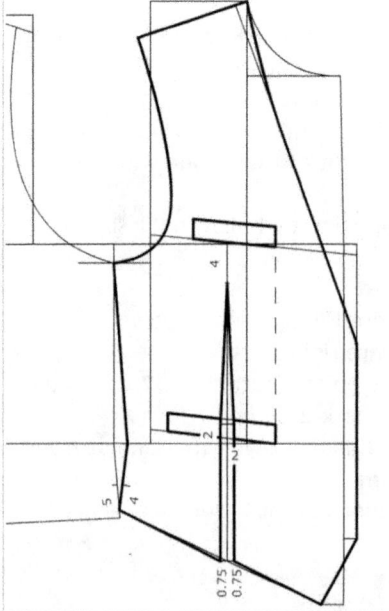

Front dart
- from chest-center-line on WL-line: mark to the left 2 cm and square up and down
- on this line from chest-line: mark down 4 cm
- on the same line from WL-line: mark up 2 cm and square left and right
- mark depth-of-dart with 0.75 cm on each side und square down each
- finish dart as shown (dart should be pointy at upper part)
- balance hem at the dart as shown

Vent
- on front pattern, at side seam from hem: mark up 4 cm
- on back pattern, at side seam from hem: mark up 5 cm
- if you do not like the vent, the side seam at the back and front should be even

Cutting
- cut front 2 x
- cut back 2 x

Instructions
- all measures are in cm
- all seams are without seam allowances

Taken measurements

	1/2	1/4	1/8	1/16
Height (*HEI*)	180	90	45	22,5	11.25
Chest (*CHE*)	102	51	25.5	12.75
Waist (*WAI*)	88	44	22
Neck (*NE*)	42

Calculated measurements

Depth of scye (*DOS*) = 1/16 *HEI* + 1/8 *CHE* = 24 cm
Waist length (*WL*) = 1/4 *HEI* = 45 cm
Neckline (*NL*) = 1/6 *NE* + 1 = 8 cm
Back width (*BW*) = 2/10 *CHE* = 20.4 cm ~ 20.5 cm
Width of scye (*WOS*) = 1/8 *CHE* = 12.75 ~ 13 cm
Chest width (*CW*) = 2/10 *CHE* + 1.5 = 21.9 ~ 22 cm
Front waist length (*FWL*) = *DOS* + 1.5 = 25.5 cm

doppel-breasted vest
Follow the instructions for the single-breasted vest as shown in picture 1 on page 29 and then continue on page 35.

Control
Compare chest-width and waist-width with the taken measurements.
The fullness at the 1/2 chest should be about 4.5 cm.
The fullness at the 1/2 waist should be about 4.5 cm.

Grainline
In the front part, the center front *CF* serves as a grainline-reference, in the back part the center-chest-line is doing this job.

Seam allowances

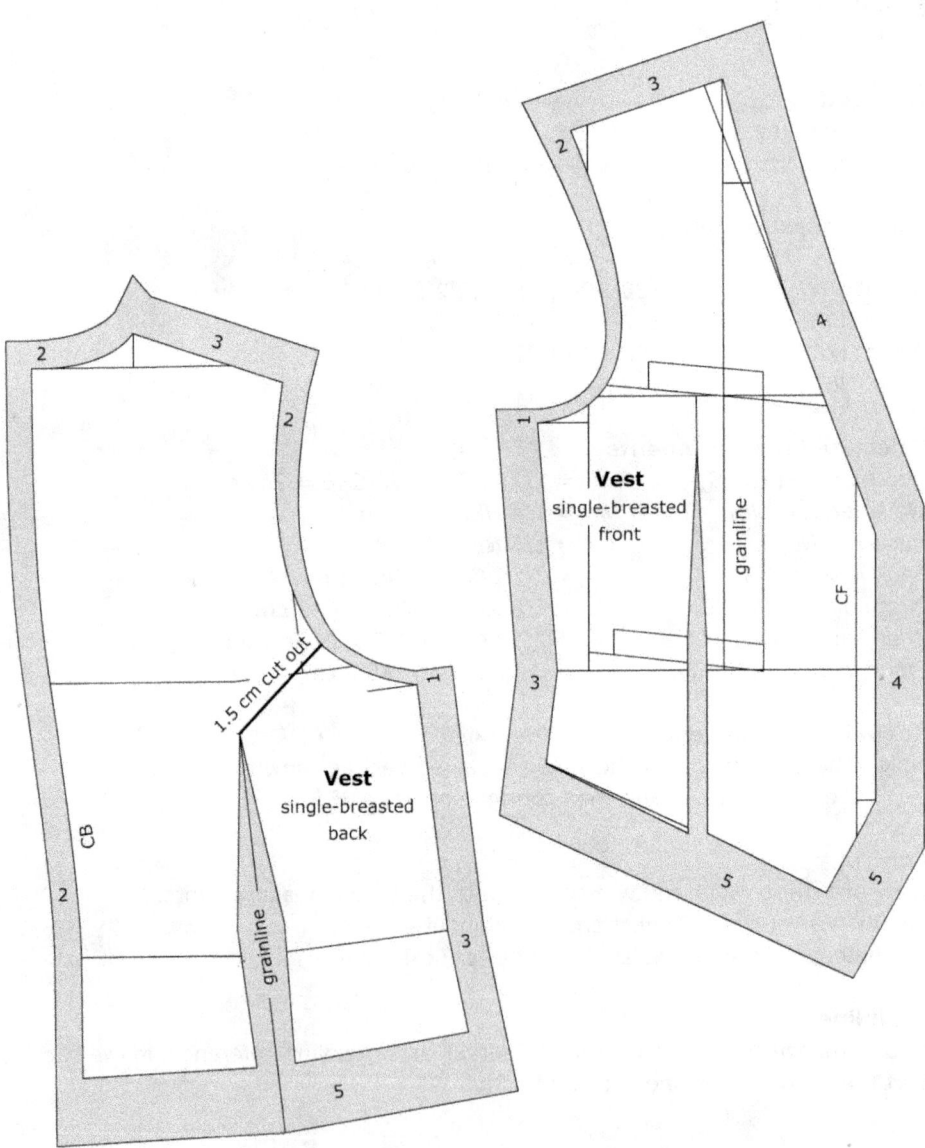

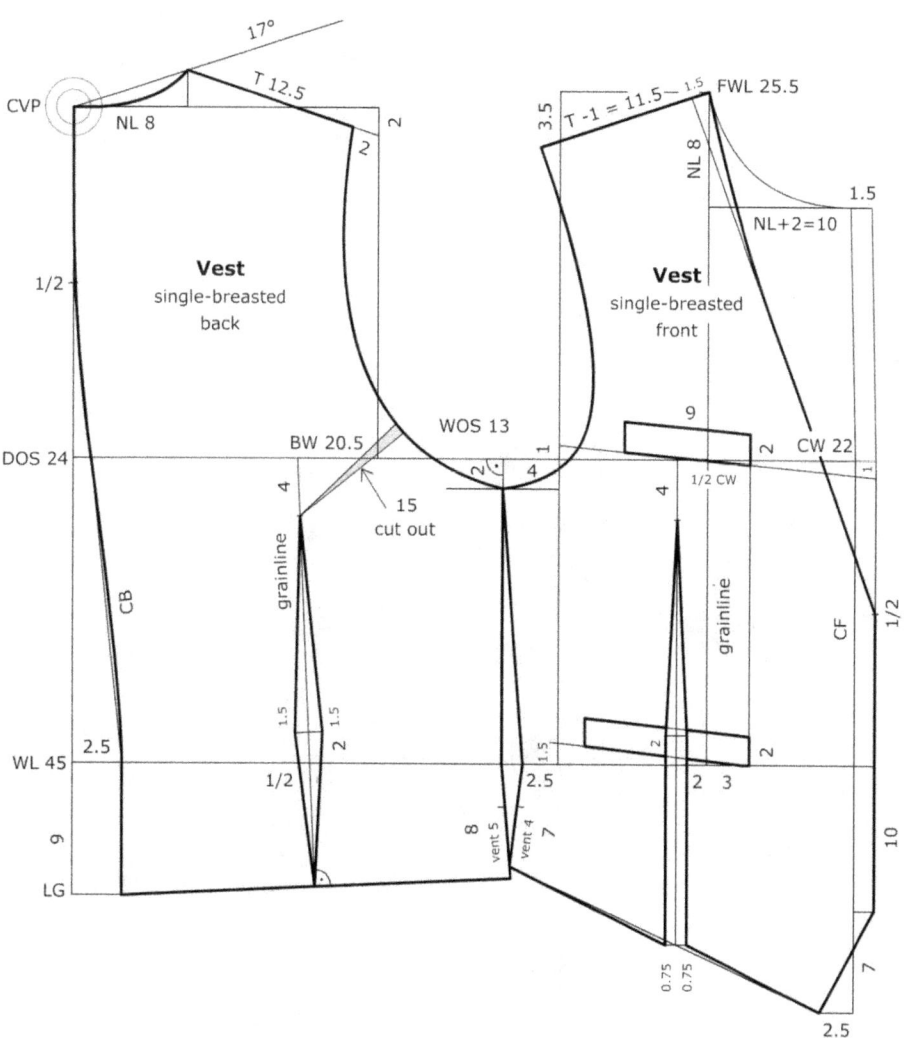

Manual for the double-breasted vest

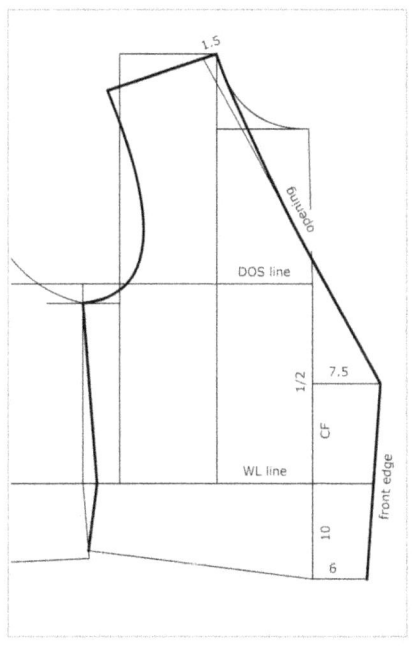

Front opening
- at the soulder: mark to the left 1.5 cm
- at *CF* between *DOS*-Linie and *WL*-line: halve the distance, square right and mark 7.5 cm
- connect both points
- hollow out the opening slightly

Front edge
- at *CF* from *WL*-line: mark down 10 cm, square right and mark 6 cm
- draw front edge

Hem
- connect lower point at *CF* with lower point at side seam

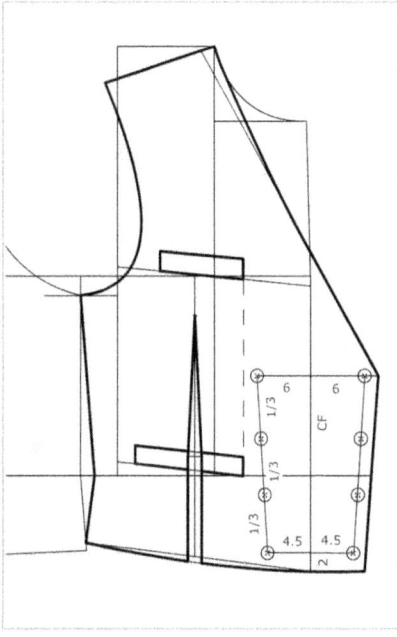

Darts and pockets
- the position of the dart and the pockets are placed in the same way as for the single-breasted vest, see page 30

Buttons
- at *CF* from hem: mark up 2 cm and square left and right
- on this line: mark to each side 4.5 cm
- at *CF* from upper line: mark to each side 6 cm
- connect the upper points to the lower points and divide the distance into three

Hem
- the shape of the hem is balanced after the darts (see page 30) have been marked

Seam allowances

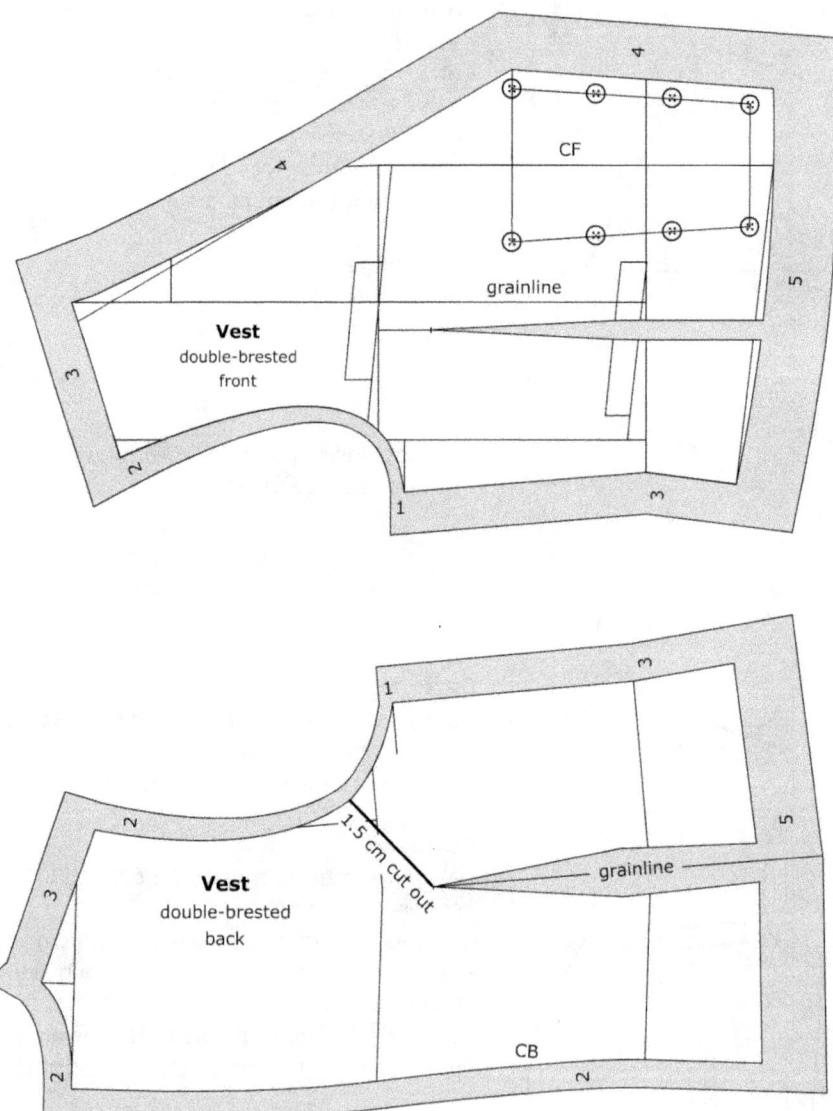

37

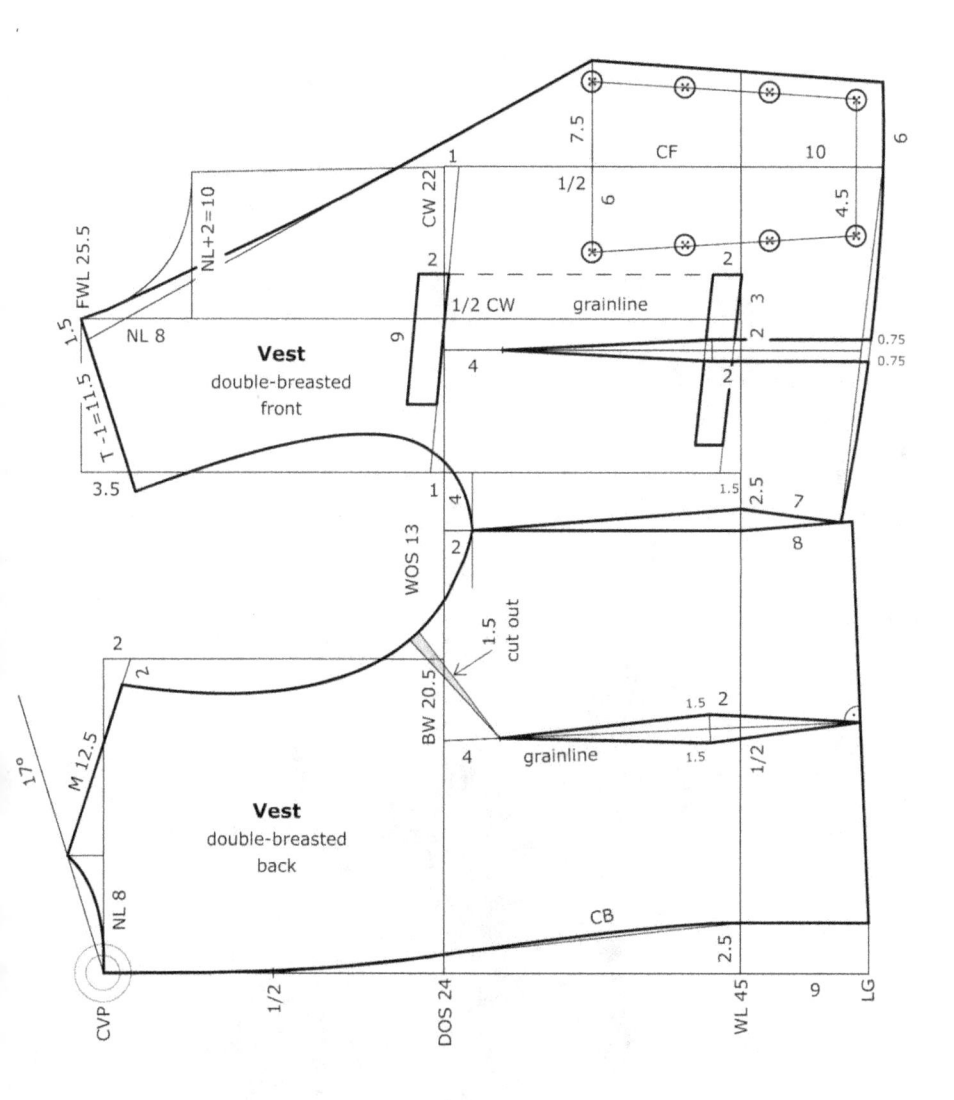

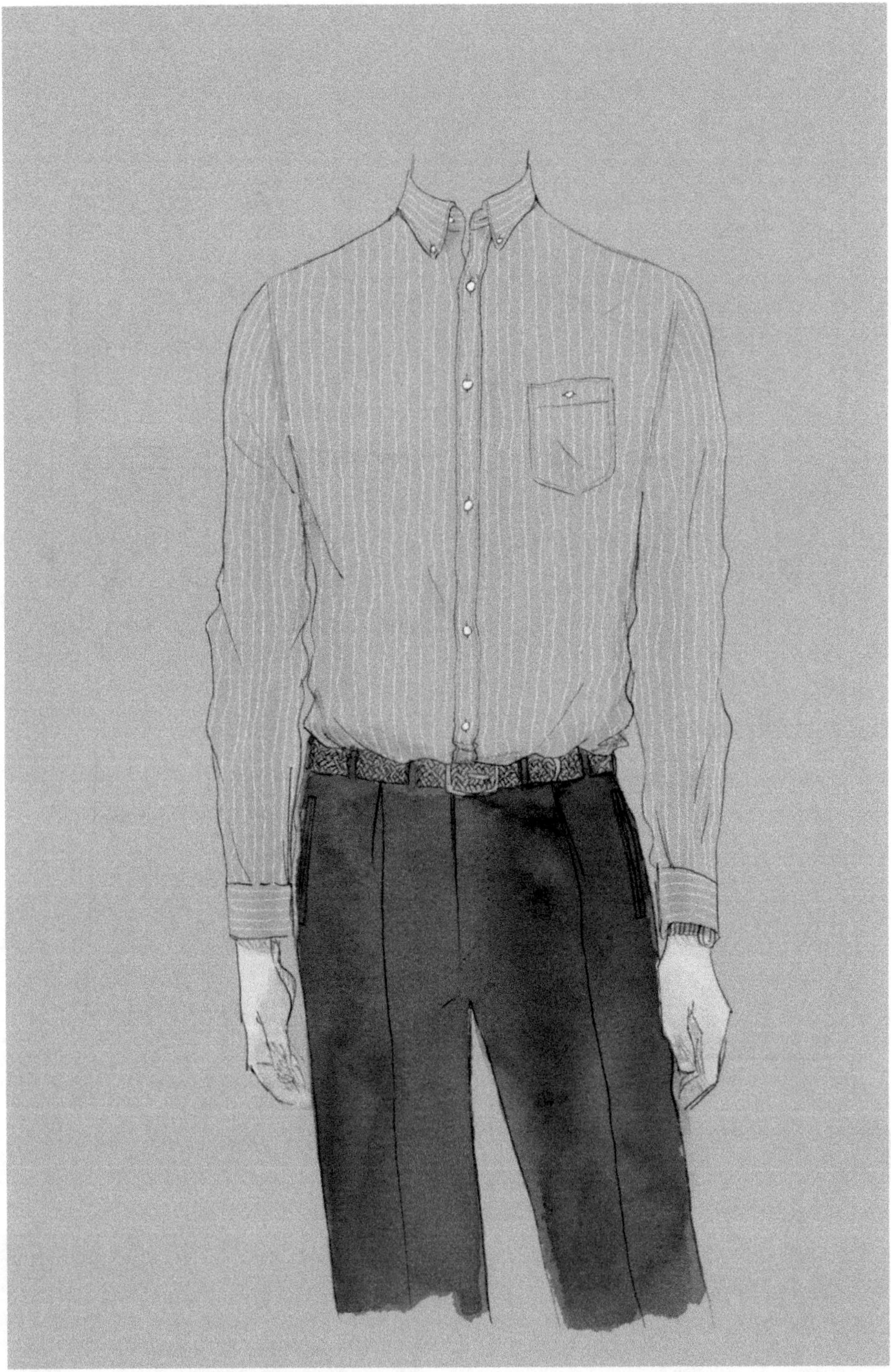

Manual for the shirt

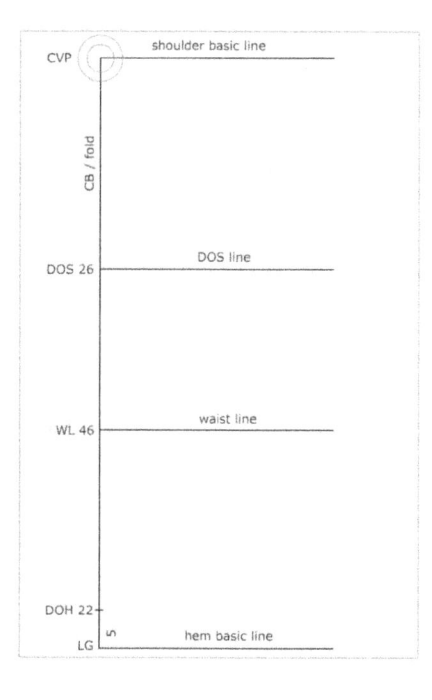

Start
- draw right angle
- vertical line is the center-back *CB* and the fold
- horizontal line is the shoulder-basic-line
- on *CB*-line from the 7th cervical-vertebra-point *CVP*: mark down depth-of-scye
  DOS = 1/16 *HEI* + 1/8 *CHE* + 3 = 26 cm
  and square right
- on *CB*-line from *CVP*: mark down waist-length *WL* = 1/4 *HEI* + 2 = 46 cm
  and square right
- on *CB*-line from *WL*: mark down depth-of-hips
  DOH = 1/8 *HEI* = 22 cm
- from *DOH*: mark down 5 cm and square right

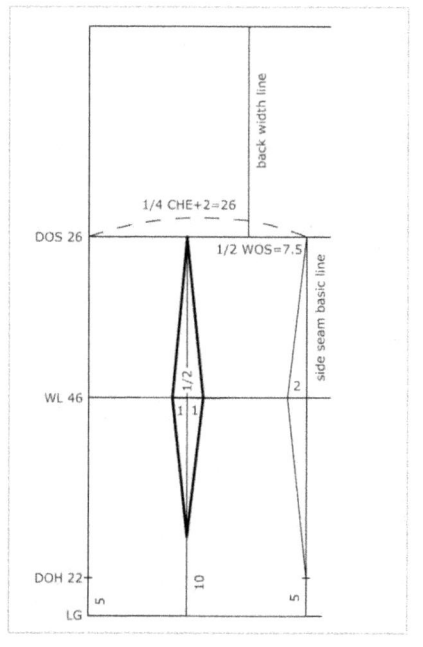

Chest width
- on *DOS*-line: mark to the right 1/4 *CHE* + 2 = 26 cm and square down

Back width
- on *DOS*-line: mark to the left 1/2 width-of-scye *WOS* = 7.5 cm and square up

Narrow waist
- from side-seam-basic-line on *WL*-line: mark to the left approx. 2 cm
- from hem-basic-line mark up 5 cm and draw side seam

Dart
- halve the distance on *WL*-line and square up and down, for the depth-of-dart mark to each side approx. 1 cm
- from hem-basic-line: mark up 10 cm and finish dart

39

The shirt

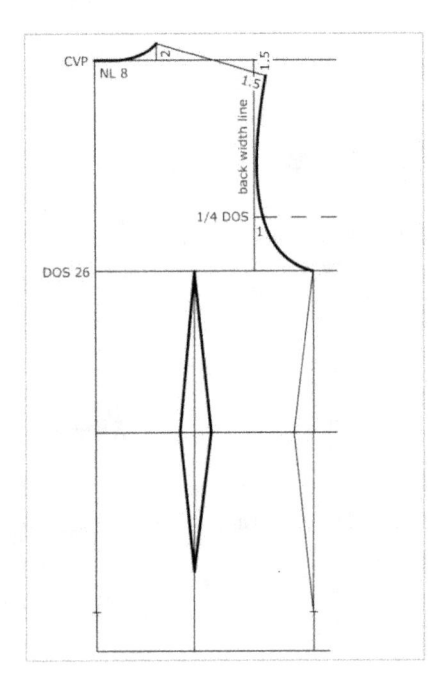

Back neckline
- from *CVP* on shoulder-basic-line: mark to the right neckline *NL* = 1/6 *NE* + 1 = 8 cm, square up and mark 2 cm
- shape neckline nicely

Shoulder
- from shoulder-basic-line on back-width-line: mark down 1.5 cm
- from upper point at neck draw shoulder-seam through previous point
- on shoulder-seam from *BW*-line: extend to the right by 1.5 cm

Back armhole
- on back-width-line: mark up 1/4 *DOS* = 6.5 cm, square right and mark 1 cm
- shape armhole nicely

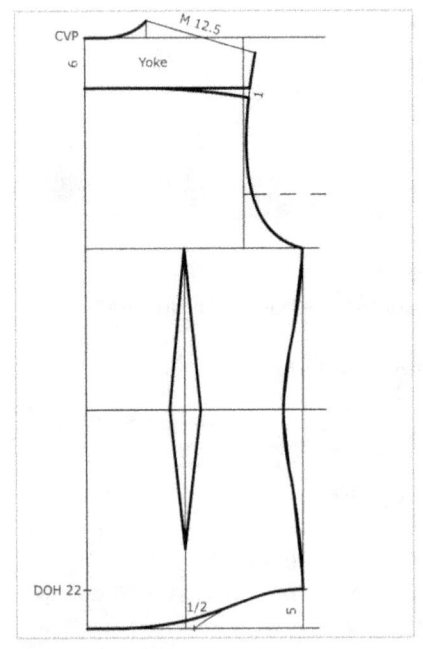

Yoke
- from *CVP* on *CB*-line: mark down 6 cm and square right
- at back-armhole from yoke-line: mark down 1 cm and shape seam nicely

Hem
- halve hem-basic-line and shape hem nicely

Side seam
- shape nicely

Shoulder
- measure width of shoulder seam *M* = approx. 12.5 cm (you will need this for the front shoulder)

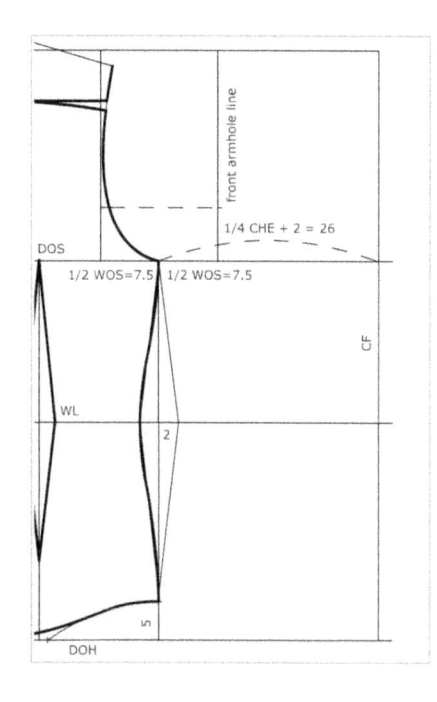

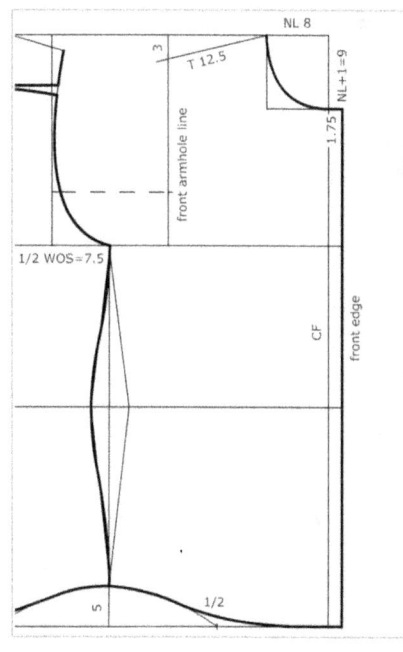

Basic frame front piece
- extend shoulder-basic-line, chest-line, WL-line and hem-basic-line

Chest
- on chest-line from side-seam-basic-line: mark to the right 1/4 CHE + 2 = 26 cm and square up and down
- this is the center-front CF

Chest width / front armhole width
- on chest-line from sideseam-basic-line: mark to the right 1/2 width-of-scye WOS = 7.5 cm and square up
- this line is the front-armhole-line

Narrow waist
- On WL-line at sideseam-basic-line: mark to the right approx ca. 2 cm and draw sideseam

Front neck
- on shoulder-basic-line from CF: mark to the left NL = 8 cm and square down
- on CF-line from the top: mark down NL + 1 = 9 cm and square left
- shape front neckline

Front shoulder
- on front-armhole-line from shoulder-basic-line: mark down 3 cm, draw shoulder seam and transfer width of back T = 12.5 cm

Center front / Front edge
- from CF: mark to the right 1.75 cm and square up and down

Hem
- halve hem-basic-line and shape hem nicely

The shirt

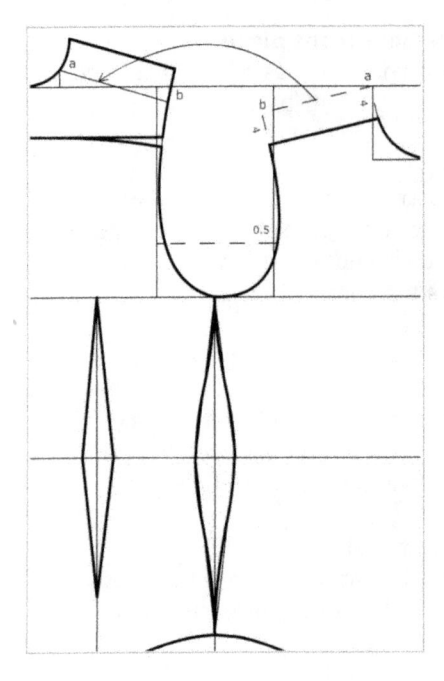

Front armhole
- at dashed line mark 0.5 cm to the right and shape armhole nicely
- measure the complete armhole (front piece, back piece and yoke)
  M = approx. 54 cm
  (you will need this flater or the sleeves)

Sideseam
- shape side seam nicely

Displace shoulder seam for yoke
- move down the soulder seam at the front part by 4 cm
- cut off that piece and stick it to the soulder-seam at the yoke
- if you do not like to displace the seam, leave it as is. This has no effect on the fit.

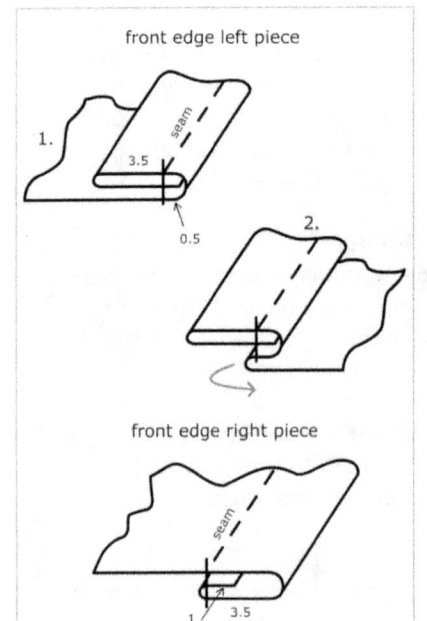

Finishing the front edge
Front edge left piece
1. Picture
- fold to the left side 3.5 cm and press
- fold again 3.5 cm and press again
- stitch with a width of 0.5 cm, so that the cutting edge is hidden inside

2. Picture
- fold back the front piece and press

Front edge right piece
- fold to the left side 1 cm and press
- fold to the left side 3.5 cm and press
- stich close to the first fold

Cutting
- cut front 2 x
- cut back in fold 1 x
- cut yoke in fold 2 x

Instructions
- all measures are in cm
- all seams are without seam allowances

Taken measurements

	1/2	1/4	1/8	1/16
Height (HEI)	176	88	44	22	11
Chest (CHE)	96	48	24	12
Waist (WAI	88	44	22
Neck (NE)	42
Sleeve lenght (SL)	62
width of cuff (WOC)	26

Calculated measurements
Depth of scye (DOS) = 1/16 HEI + 1/8 CHE + 3 = 26 cm
Waist length (WL) = 1/4 HEI + 2 = 46 cm
Depth of hips (DOH) = 1/8 HEI = 22 cm
Neckline (NL) = 1/6 NE + 1 = 8 cm
Width of scye (WOS) = 1/8 CHE + 3 = 15 cm

Armhole
Measured after drafting = approx. 54 cm

Control
Compare width of chest, width of waist and width of hips in the pattern with the taken measurements.
If the waist is too tight: draw the side seam less narrow and, if necessary, do the back part without the darts or draw them in smaller.

The fullness at the 1/2 chest should be about 4 cm.
The fullness at the 1/2 waist should be about 4 cm.

Grainline
CF and CB serve as a grainline reference.

Seam allowances

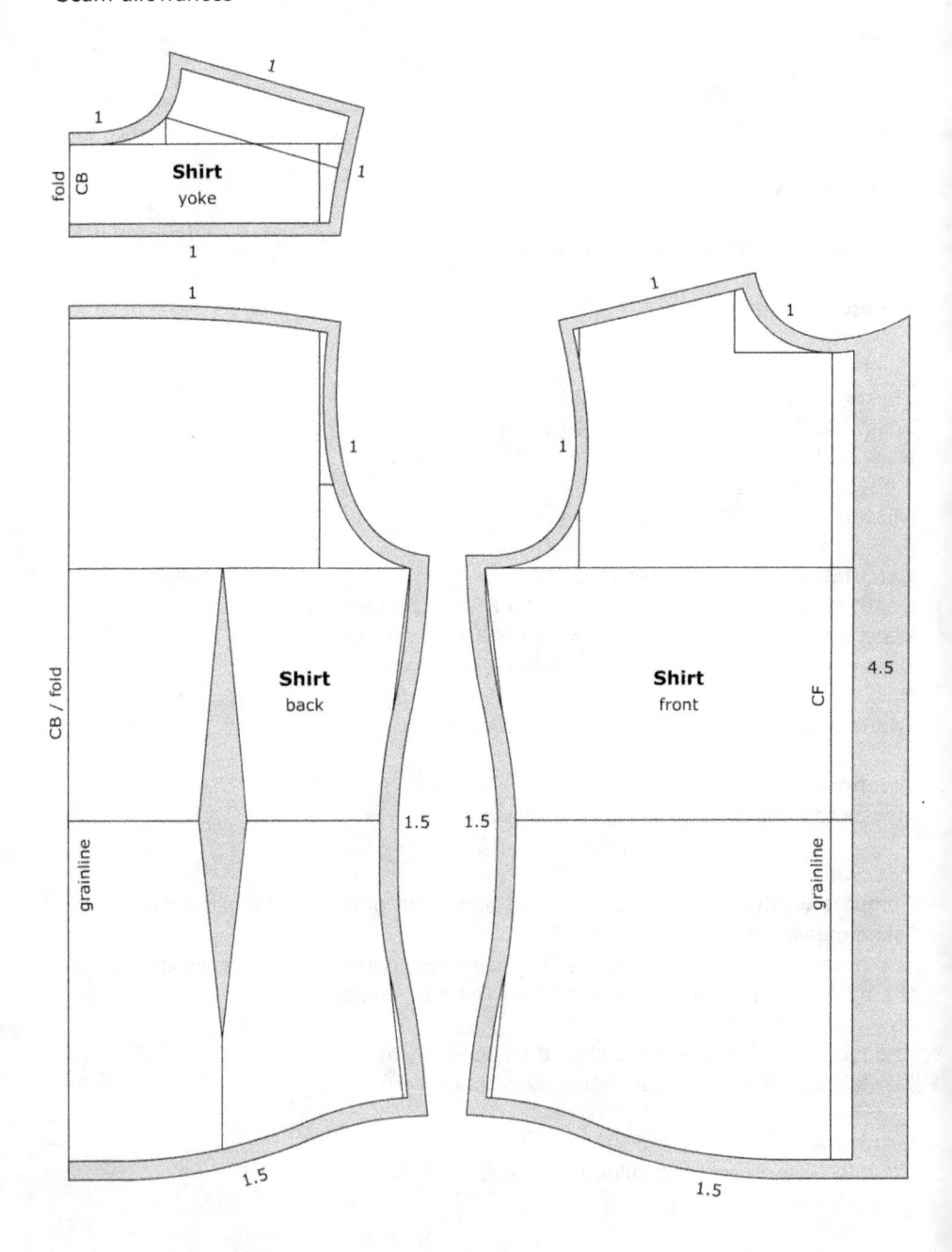

45

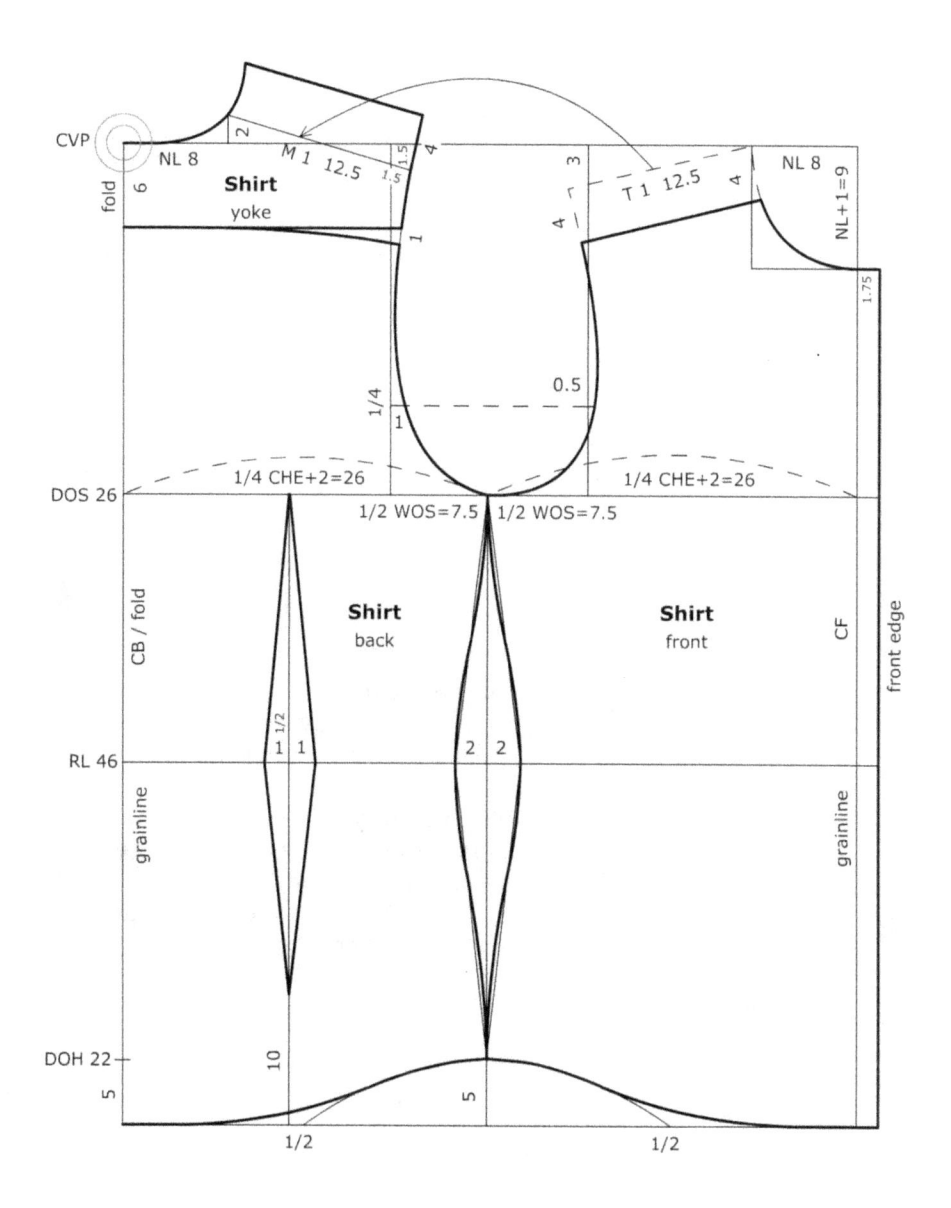

Manual for the shirt sleeve

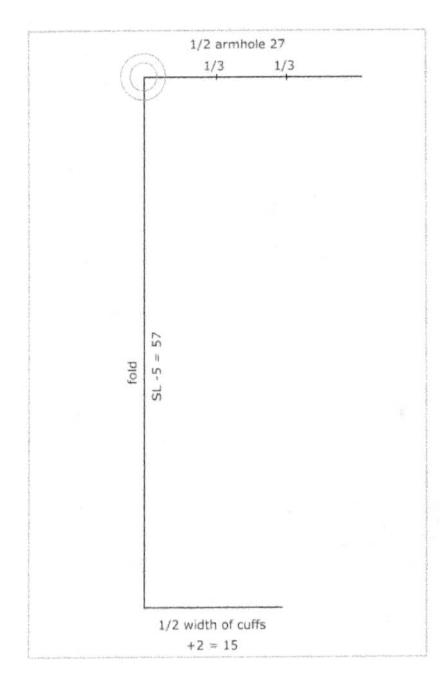

Start

(for measurements see page 43)

- draw right angle
- on horizontal line: mark to the right 1/2 armhole = 27 cm
- divide this distance into three

- on vertical line: mark down sleeve-lenght *SL* - 5 = 57 cm and square right
- on this line: mark to the right 1/2 width of the cuffs + 2 cm (for pleats) = 15 cm
- vertical line is the fold and serves as the grainline

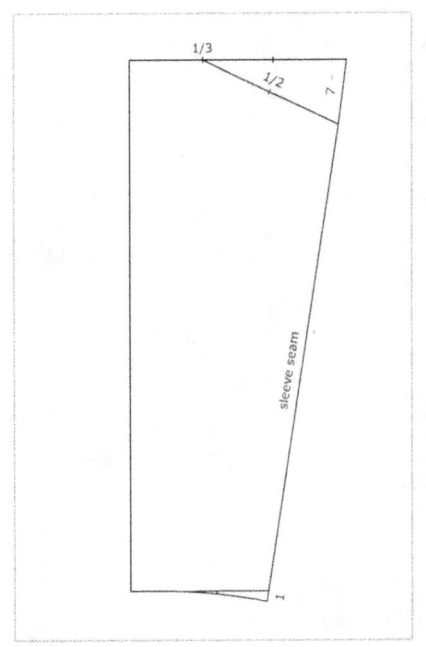

Sleeve seam
- connect the right outer points on the upper and lower horizontal lines

Sleeve head
- from upper horizontal line at sleeve-seam: mark down 7 cm
- connect this point with the first point on the upper horizontal line and halve this distance

Seam at wrist
- from lower horizontal line at sleeve seam: mark down 1 cm
- shape cuff seam nicely

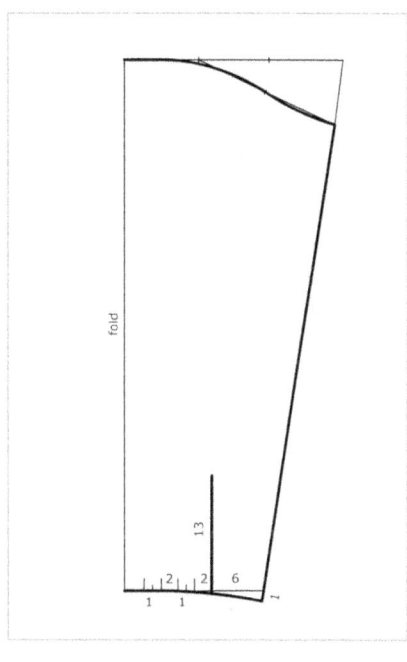

Sleeve head
- shape sleeve-head nicely

Sleeve vent
- at seam for cuffs from sleeve seam: mark to the left 6 cm, square up and mark the vent with 13 cm

Folds
- from vent: for 1. pleat mark to the left 2 cm and mark depth of pleat (2 x 1 cm)
- from this point: for 2. pleat mark again to the left 2 cm and mark depth of pleat (2 x 1 cm)

- see also bigger pattern on page 49

Cutting
cut in fold 2 x

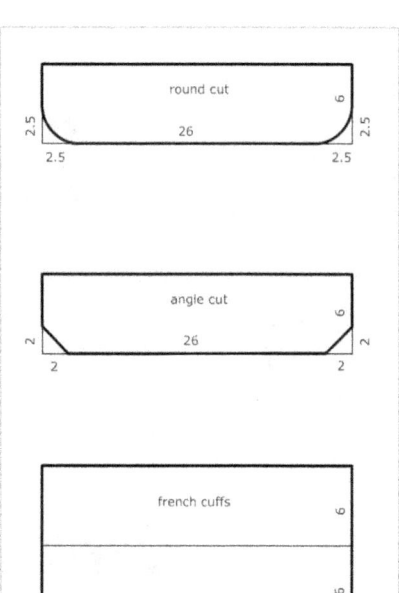

Round cut cuffs
- draw rectangle with a height of 6 cm and a width of 26 cm
- at the lower corners mark 2.5 cm each and draw this corners round

Angle cut cuffs
- draw rectangle with a height of 6 cm and a width of 26 cm
- at the lower corners mark 2 cm each and draw the diagonals

French cut cuffs
- draw rectangle with a height of 12 cm and a width of 26 cm
- divide vertical line into half and square right

Cutting
- decide for one variation and cut 4 x

Seam allowances

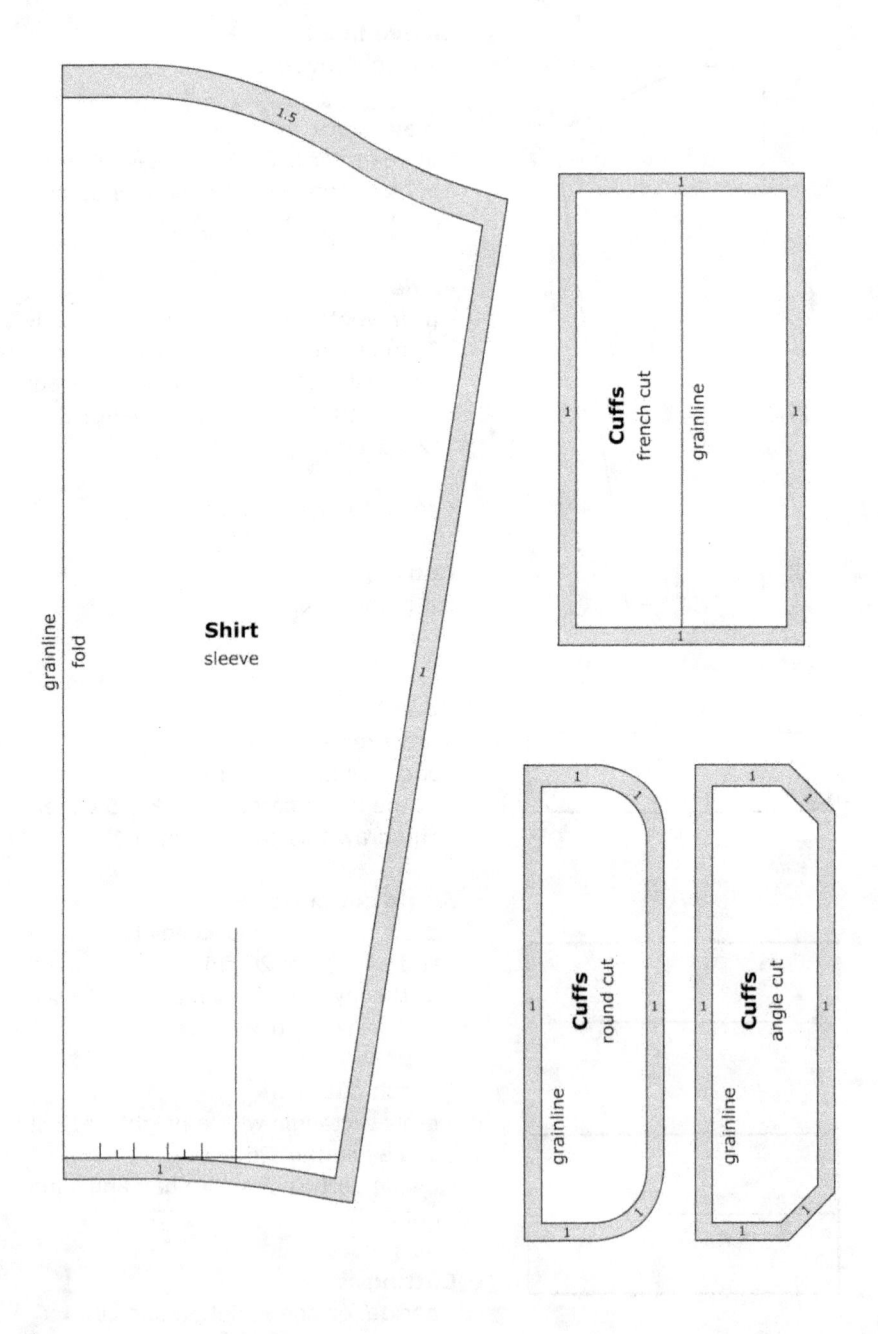

1/2 armhole 27

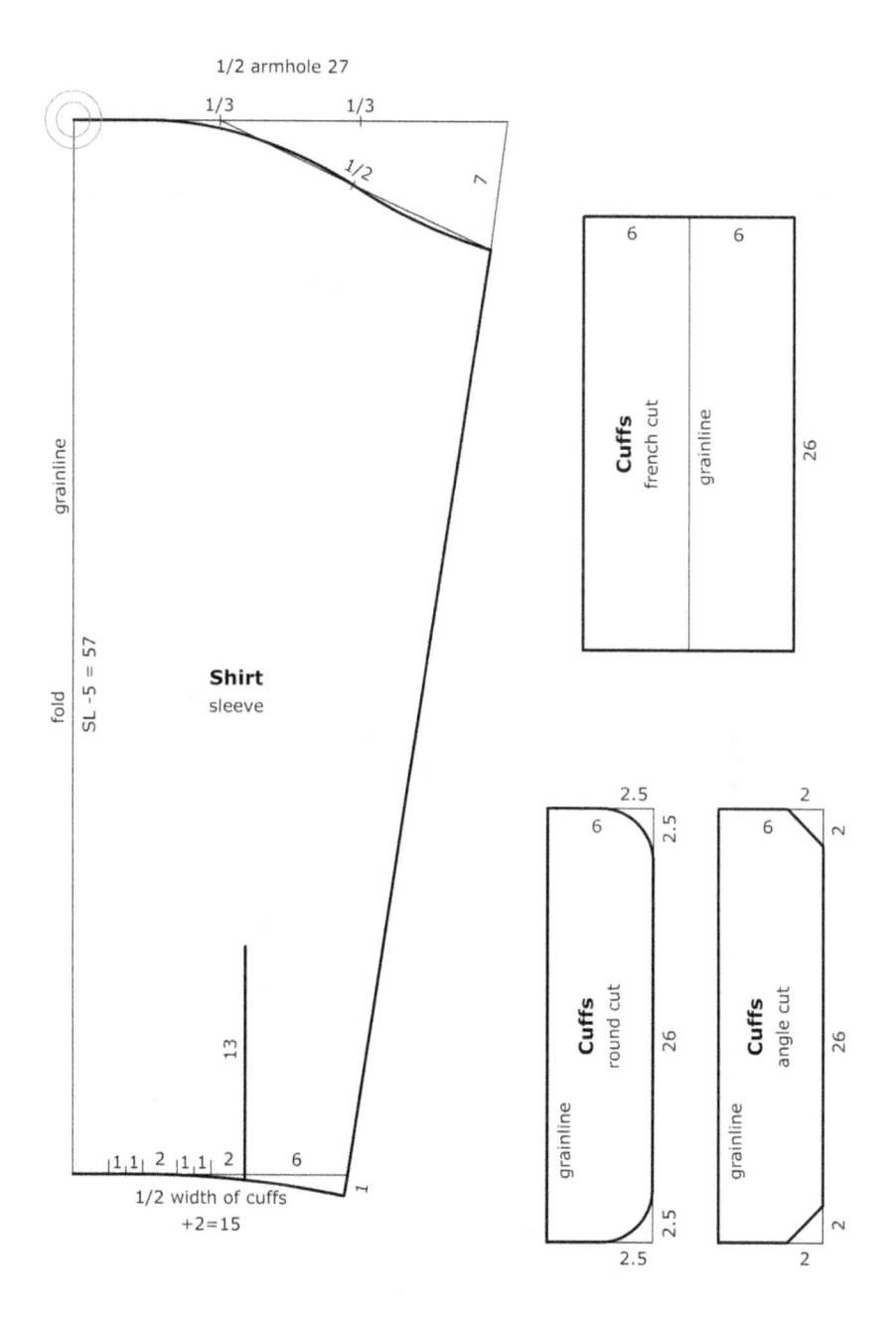

1/3 1/3

1/2

7

grainline

fold

SL -5 = 57

Shirt
sleeve

13

|1,1| 2 |1,1| 2   6

1

1/2 width of cuffs
+2=15

Cuffs
french cut

6   6

grainline

26

Cuffs
round cut

2.5
6   2.5

grainline

26

2.5

Cuffs
angle cut

2
6   2

grainline

26

2

2

Manual for the tuxedo (wing) collar

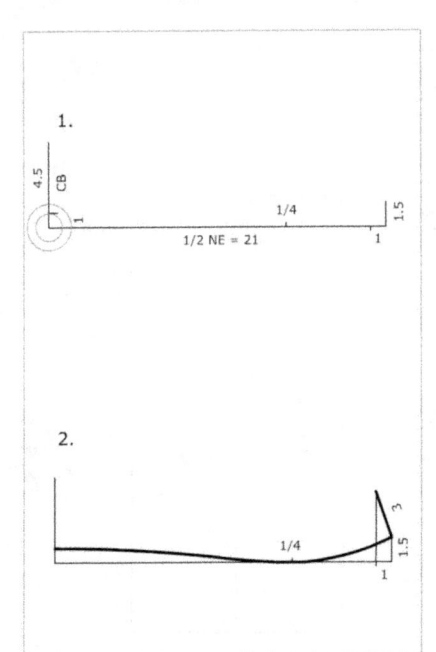

1. Start
(For measurements see page 43)

- draw right angle
- on horizontal line: mark to the right 1/2 neck NE = 21 cm and divide this distance into four
- mark to the right 1 cm, square up and mark 1.5 cm
- on vertical line at CB: mark up 1 cm
- from here mark up 4.5 cm

2.
- shape collar-seam nicely as shown
- at 1 cm point: square up
- from 1.5 cm point: draw diagonal line with length of 3 cm touching previous line

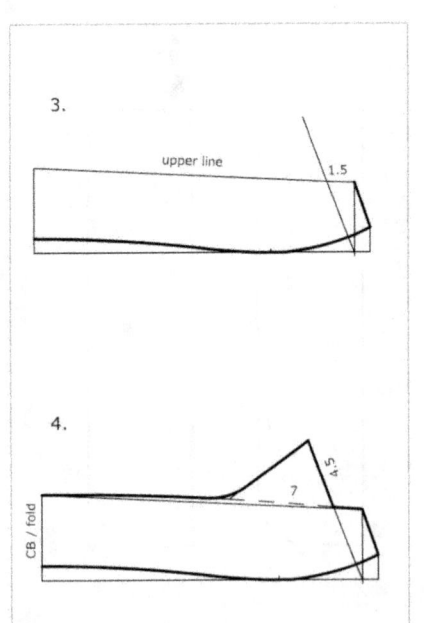

3. collar tip
- draw upper line and mark to the left 1.5 cm
- draw diagonal line

4.
- for the tip of the collar, mark up 4.5 cm and mark to the left 7 cm as shown
- connect both points
- the tip is turned down at the dotted line after sewing

Cutting
cut in fold 2 x

Manual for the english cutaway collar

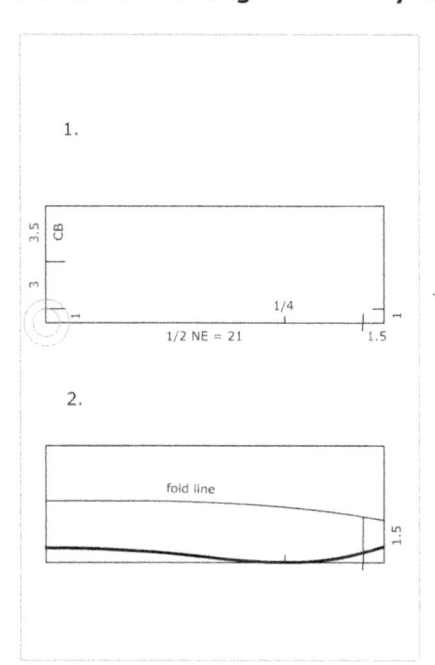

1. Start
- draw right angle
- on horizontal line: mark to the right 1/2 neck *NE* = 21 cm and divide this distance into four
- mark to the right 1.5 cm, square up and mark 1 cm
- on vertical line at *CB*: mark up 1 cm
- from here mark up 3 cm
- from here mark up 3.5 cm and square right

2.
- shape collar-seam nicely as shown
- up front: mark up 1.5 cm
- shape collar-fold-line nicely

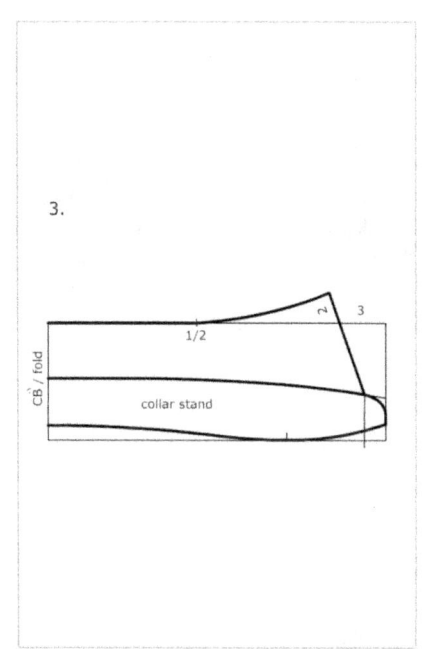

3. Collar tip
- on upper line from up front: mark to the left 3 cm and halve the remaining distance
- draw in diagonal line and mark up 2 cm
- finish the collar as shown

Cutting
cut collarstand in fold 2 x
cut turndown in fold 2 x

Instruction
The collar also can be cut out in one piece

Manual for the classic collar

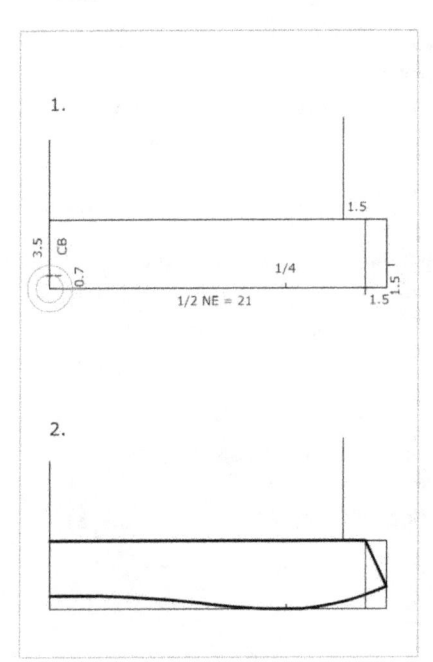

1. Start
- draw right angle
- on vertical line at *CB*: mark up 0.7 cm
- from here mark up 3.5 cm and square right
- on horizontal line: mark to the right 1/2 neck *NE* = 21 cm and divide this distance into four
- mark to the right 1.5 cm, square up and mark 1.5 cm
- on upper line: mark to the left 1.5 cm and square up

2.
- finish the collarstand as shown
- up front: draw in diagonal line

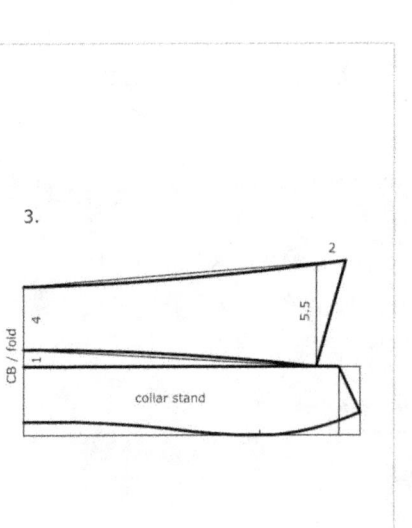

3. Collar tip
- on vertical line at *CB*: mark up 1 cm
- from here mark up 4 cm

- up front on vertical line: mark up 5.5 cm
- connect this point with upper point at center-back *CB* and extend this line forward by 2 cm

- finish the collar as shown

Cutting
cut collarstand in fold 2 x
cut turn down in fold 2 x

Instructions
To draw other variants of the collar tip, you only need to vary their skew. (See also the skewness of the collar tips of the english cutaway and the classic collar) This allows you to create a variety of different collar models.

The basis for this is the draft of the classic collar.

Seam allowances

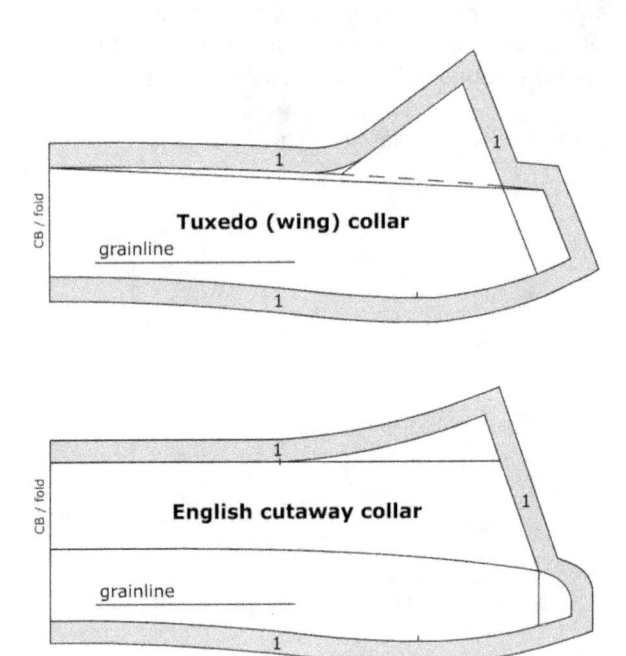

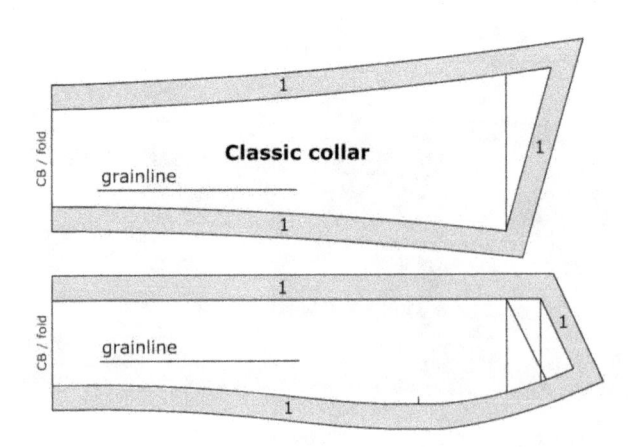

Tuxedo (wing) collar
grainline

English cutaway collar
grainline

Classic collar
grainline

grainline

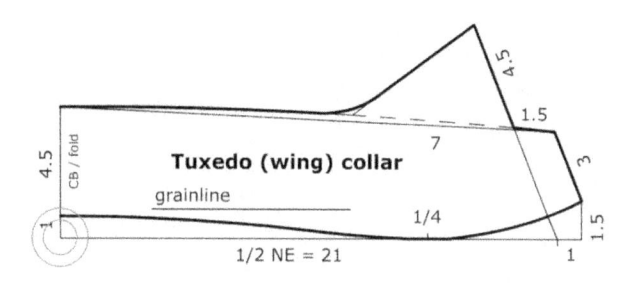

Tuxedo (wing) collar

- 4.5 CB/fold
- grainline
- 1/2 NE = 21
- 7
- 4.5
- 1.5
- 3
- 1.5
- 1/4
- 1

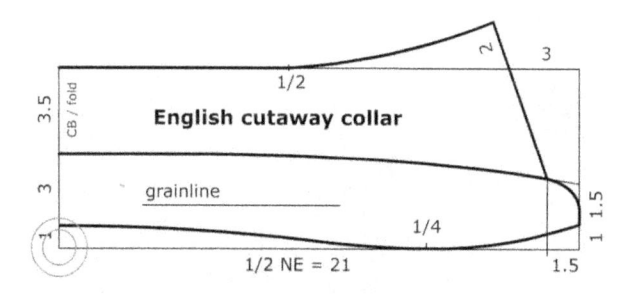

English cutaway collar

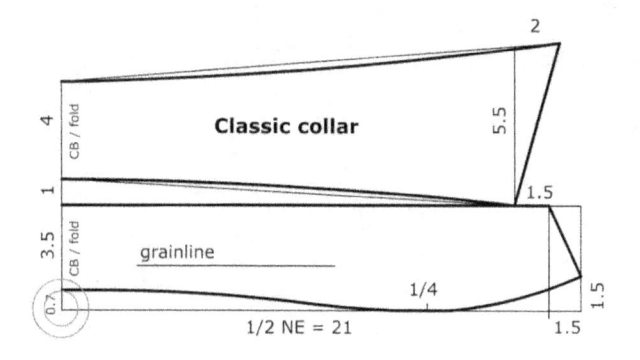

- 3.5 CB/fold
- 3
- grainline
- 1/2 NE = 21
- 1/2
- 1/4
- 2
- 3
- 1.5
- 1
- 1.5

Classic collar

- 4 CB/fold
- 1
- 3.5 CB/fold
- grainline
- 1/2 NE = 21
- 0.7
- 1/4
- 2
- 5.5
- 1.5
- 1.5
- 1.5

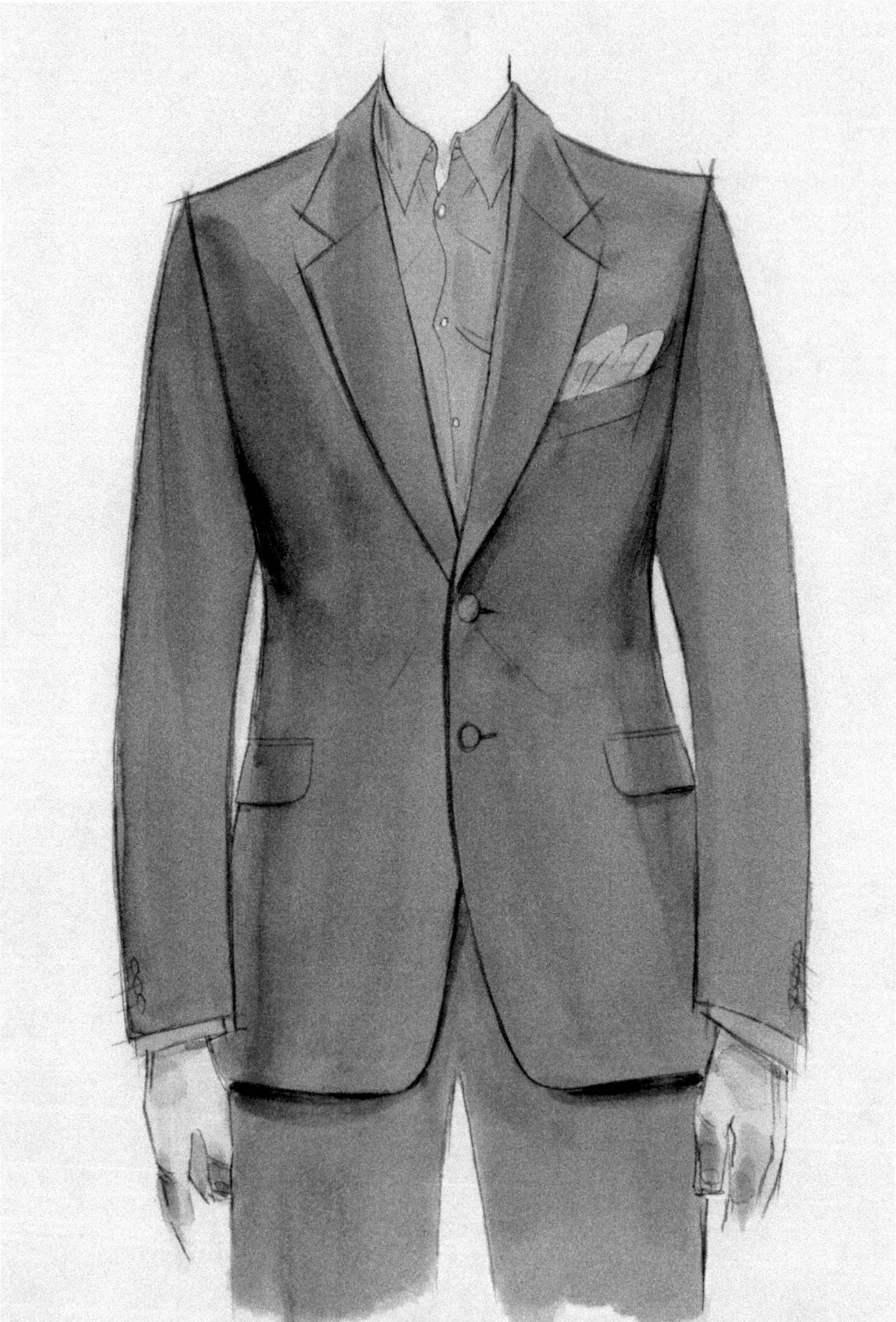

Manual for the single-breasted jacket

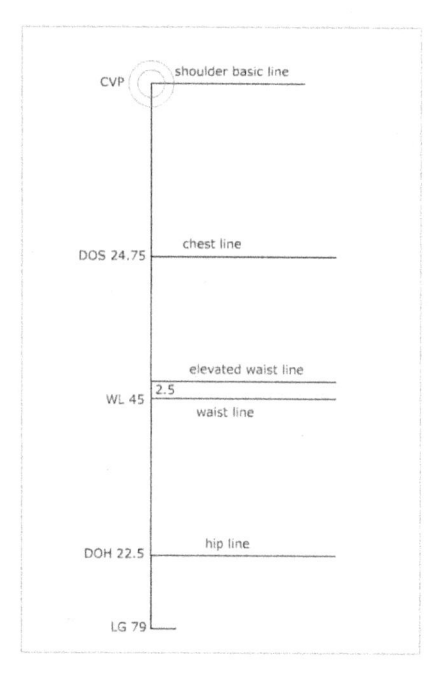

Start
- draw right angle
- Vertical line is the center-back-basic-line
- horizontal line is the shoulder-basic-line
- at center-back-basic-line from the 7th cervical-vertebra-point *CVP:* mark down $DOS = 1/16\ HEI + 1/8\ CHE = 24.75$ cm and square right
- from *CVP*: mark down waist-length $WL = 1/4\ HEI = 45$ cm and square right
- at center-back-basic-line from *WL*-line: mark up 2.5 cm and square right, this is the elevated waist
- at center-back-basic-line from *WL*: mark down $DOH = 1/8\ HEI = 22.5$ cm and square right
- at center-back-basic-line from *CVP*: mark down length $LG = 1/8\ HEI \times 3.5 = 79$ cm and square right

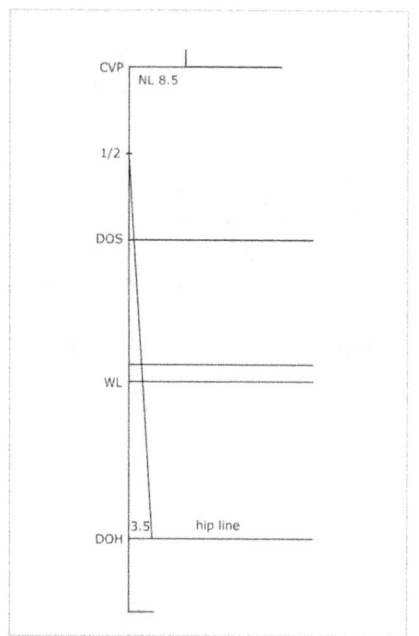

Back seam
- on center-back-basic-line: halve the distance between *CVP* and *WL*
- at *HIP*-line from *CB*-basic-line: mark to the right 3.5 cm and connect this point with previous point

Neck/Shoulder
- at shoulder-basic-line from *CVP*: mark to the right neckline $NL = 1/6\ NE + 1.5 = 8.5$ cm and square up

The single-breasted jacket

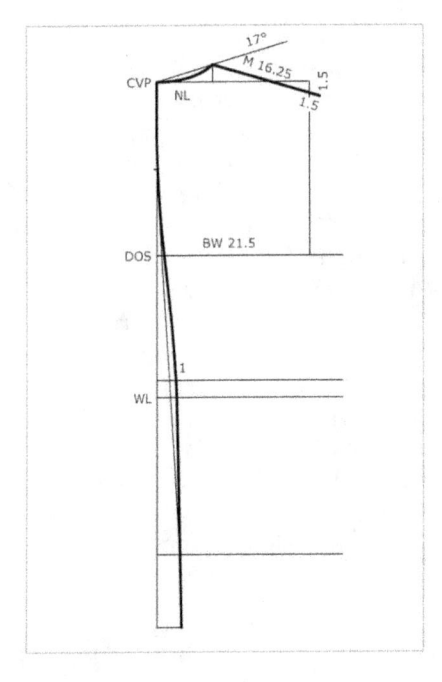

Back seam
- at line of elevated waist: mark to the right 1 cm
- shape back-seam nicely
- the back-seam is also the center-back *CB*

Shoulder
- at chest-line from *CB*: mark to the right back-width *BW* = 1/10 *CHE* + 10.5 = 21.5 cm and square up (attention: see also calculation of *BW* on page 65)
- from *CVP*: create 17° angle to the up right
- from shoulder-basic-line at *BW*-line: mark down 1.5 cm and connect with upper point at the neckline
- at shoulder from *BW*-line: extend shoulder-seam to the right by 1.5 cm and measure *M* = 16.25 cm (you will need this for the front shoulder)

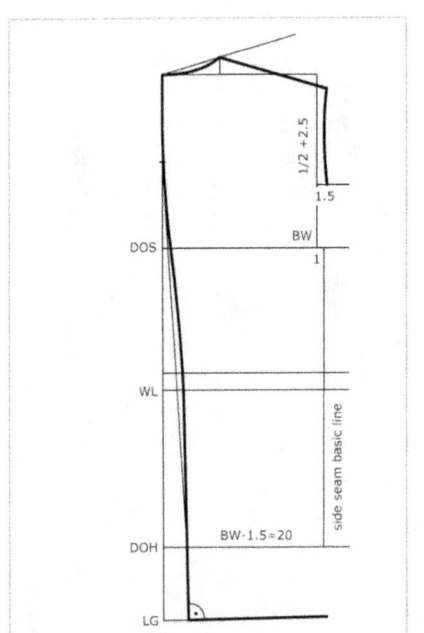

Scye / Armhole
- on *BW*-line from shoulder: mark down half the distance + 2.5 cm, square right and mark 1.5 cm
- shape back-armhole nicely

Preperation for side seam
- on chest-line from *BW*-line: mark to the right 1 cm (to hide the sides eam under the sleeve)
- on *HIP*-line from *CB*: mark to the right *BW* - 1.5 = 20 cm
- Ccnnect this point with previous point, this defines the sidesseam-basic-line
- at *LG* from *CB*: draw right angle to the right

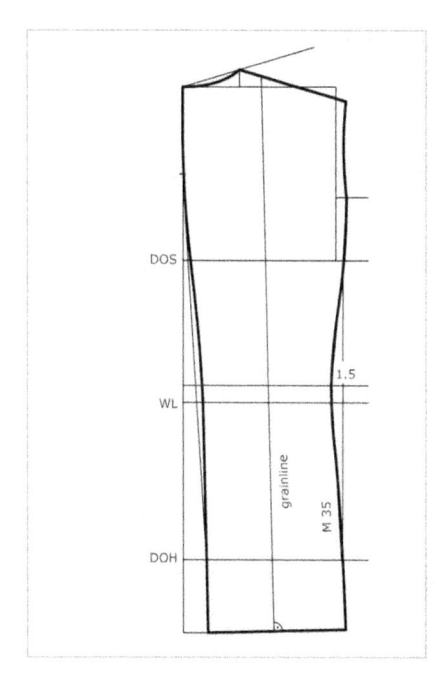

Side seam
- on elevated waist from side-seam-basic-line: mark to the left 1.5 cm
- shape side seam nicely
- on side seam from elevated waist: measure down to LG, M = approx. 36 cm (you will need this for the side part)

Grainline
- draw in a right angle to the lenght

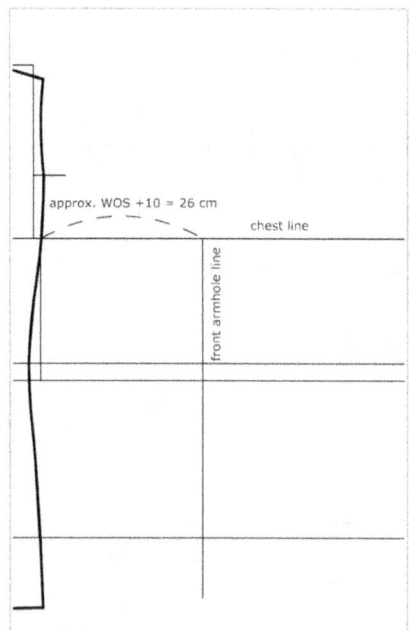

Extend lines for front and side part
- extend chest-line (also known as DOS-line), elevated waist-line, waist-line and hip-line to the right
- on chest-line: mark to the right WOS + approx. 10 = 26 cm and square down (the 10 cm are chosen at random to get enough space to the back)
- this is the front-armhole-line

The single-breasted jacket

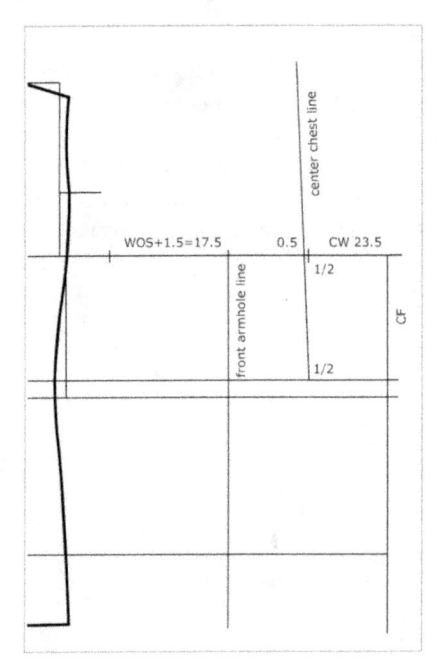

Width of scye
- on chest-line from front-armhole-line: mark to the left
  $WOS = 1/8\ CHE + 2.5 = 16$ cm $+ 1.5$
  (**for the inclination of the side part**, see page 65) $= 17.5$ cm

Chest width
- on chest-line from front-armhole-line: mark to the right chest-width
  $CW = 2/10\ CHE + 2 = 23.5$ cm and square down
- this is the center-front CF
- halve CW and mark to the left 0.5 cm (this helps for a better fit at the shoulder)
- halve distance at elevated waist-line
- connect both points as shown
- this line defines the center-chest-line

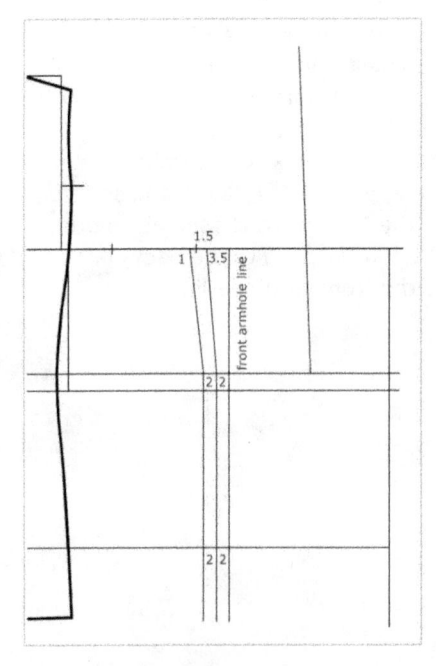

Side part
- on chest-line from front-armhole-line: mark to the left 3.5 cm
- from this point mark to the left: 1.5 cm for **the inclination of the side part** (see explanation on page 65)
- and from this point: mark to the left 1 cm (the ammount from the displaced side seam at the back)

- on elevated waist-line from front-armhole-line: mark to the left 2 cm
- from this point: mark to the left 2 cm

- on hip-line from front-armhole-line: mark to the left 2 cm
- from this point mark to the left 2 cm
- connect all points as shown

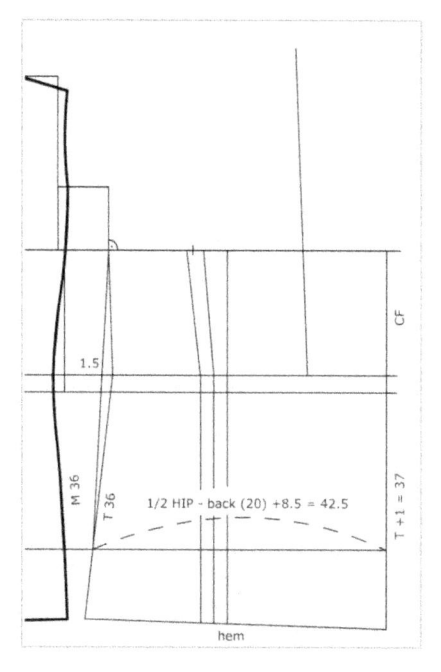

Side seam
- on hip-line from *CF*: mark to the left 1/2 *HIP* - 20 cm (width of lower back) + 8.5 (fullness and space between front- and side-part) = 42.5 cm
- connect this point with *WOS*-point on chest-line
- on elevated waist-line: mark to the right 1.5 cm and draw sideseam
- on chest-line from sideseam: square up to the line coming from the back part
- at back side seam from elevated waist: measure distance to length *M* = approx. 36 cm and transfer to front side seam *T* = 36 cm
- at *CF* from elevated waist: mark down this distance + 1 = 37 cm
- connect both points at length

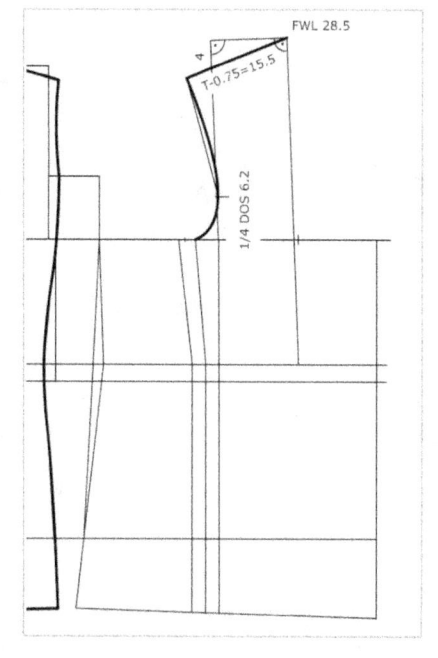

Front armhole
- on chest-line from center-chest-line: mark up front-waist-length *FWL* = *DOS* + 3.5 = approx. 28.5 cm (see also calculation on page 65)
- from this point: square left
- from this line: square down to crossing point of chest-line and front-armhole-line
- on this line from chest-line: mark up 1/4 *DOS* = 6.2 cm

Shoulder
- at front-armhole-line from the top: mark down 4 cm
- draw shoulder seam and transfer length of back-shoulder-seam - 0.75 cm = 15.5 cm
- shape front armhole nicely

The single-breasted jacket

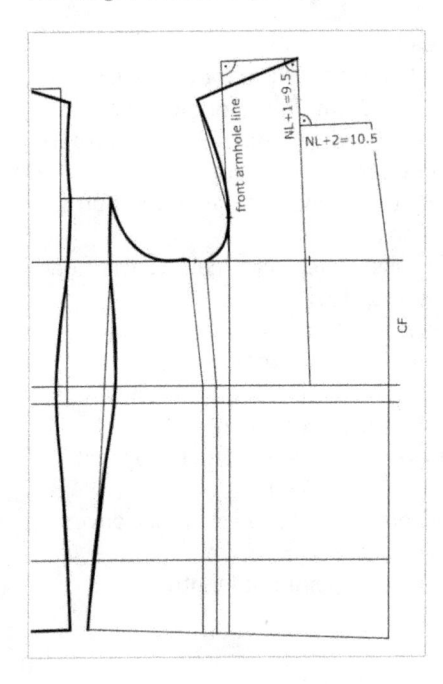

Side part armhole
- shape armhole of side part nicely

Sideseam
- shape sideseam nicely
- side seam is without any seam allowance

Neckline
- on center-line from shoulder: mark down neckline $NL = 1/6 \ NE + 1 = 9.5$ cm, square right and mark $NL + 2 = 10.5$ cm
- connect this point with CF on chest-line
- shape front neckline nicely

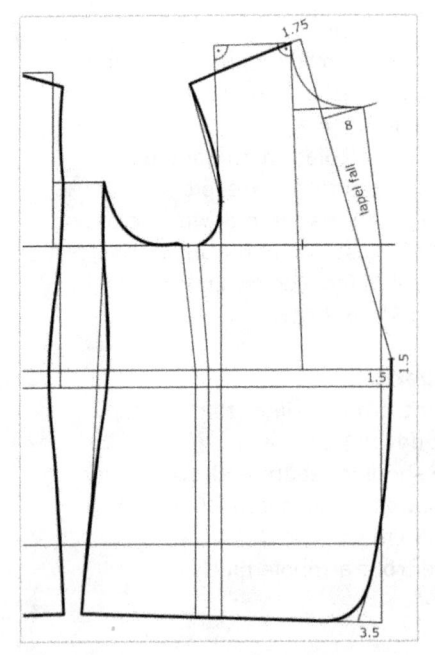

Lapel fall
- extend shoulder-line to the right and mark 1.75 cm
- on elevated waist from CF: mark to the right 1.5 cm, square up and mark 1.5 cm
- connect this point with previous point at shoulder-line
- on lapel-fall: square to the right to tip of CF/neckline
- on this line: mark 8 cm for lapel-width

Lower front edge
- on hem-line from CF: mark to the left 3.5 cm
- draw front edge with slightly rounded line
- shape curve at lower front edge as shown

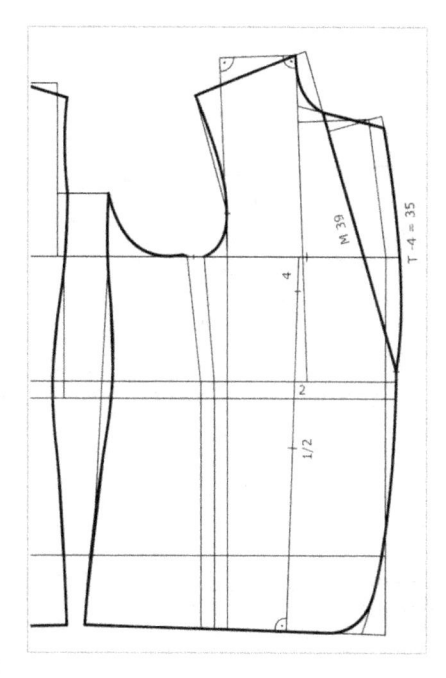

Lapel
- shape edge of lapel with a slight curve
- measure lapel-fall M = approx. 39 cm and transfer T this measure - 4 = 35 cm to the lapel-edge
- from lapel tip at CF: draw line to top of lapel-fall

Dart
- on elevated waist from center-line: mark to the left 2 cm
- at hem-line square up through previous point
- halve this dart-line between chest-line and hem as shown
- on dart-line from chest-line: mark down 4 cm

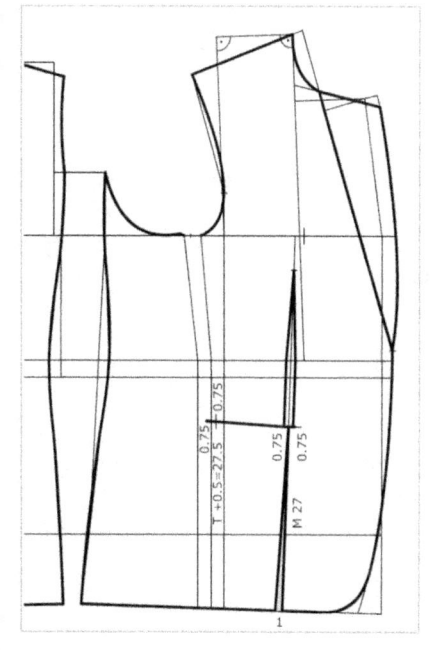

Dart
- from end of dart to hem: measure length of lower dart-line M = approx. 27 cm and transfer length $T + 0.5$ = 27.5 cm to side-part-seam
- mark depth of dart with 0.75 cm on each side and finish dart as shown
- draw pocket-opening as shown
- on this line from side-part-line: mark 0.75 cm to each side (the same amount as marked at the darts)

Rotate lower front piece
- at hem from dart-line: mark to the left 1 cm and draw up to the pocket opening
- for a better shape, this part will be cut out and put together. This rotates the lower front part

The single-breasted jacket

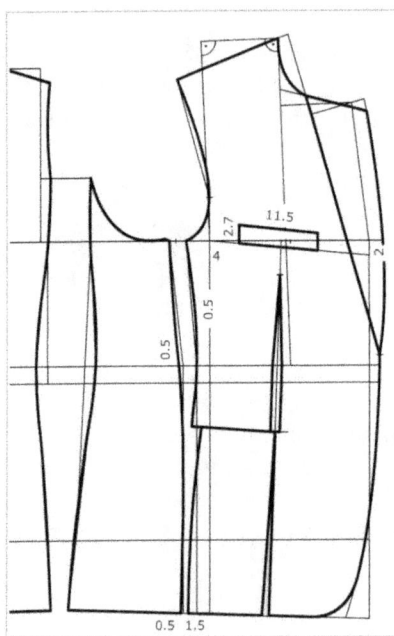

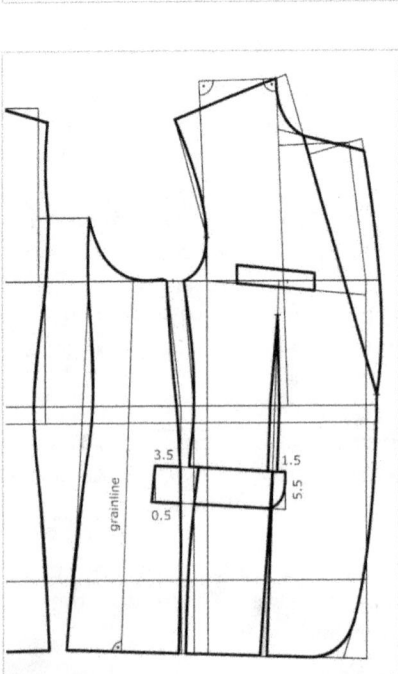

Breast pocket
- on chest-line from *CF*: mark down 2 cm and draw line to crossing of front-armhole-line and chest-line
- on this line from front-armhole-line: mark to the right approx. 4 cm and square up
- mark pocket opening with approx. 11.5 cm and square up
- mark heigth of welt pocket with approx. 2.7 cm

Side-part-seam
- on hem-line: mark to the left 1.5 and 0.5 cm (see also bigger pattern on p. 67)

Narrow waist
- at side-part-seam: mark approx. 0.5 cm to each side (see also p. 67)
- shape side-part-seam as shown

Flap pocket
- at pocket opening from dart: mark to the right 1.5 cm and square down
- extend line of pocket opening to the left and mark approx. 3.5 cm from side-part-seam (the pocket opening should be around 15 - 17 cm)
- mark flap width with approx. 5.5 cm, the front curve should be similar to the curve at the front edge
- the lower lenght of the flap is around 0.5 cm longer then the upper line

Grainline
- at the front part the center of the dart defines the grainline
- at the side-part square up from the hem

Cutting
- cut front-, side- and back-part 2 x each

Instructions
- all measures are in cm. The fullness at the 1/2 chest, 1/2 waist and 1/2 hips should be 5.5 cm
- 0.75 cm seam allowances are included (sewing machine foot width) at the shoulder seam, the entire armhole and the side-part-seam, all other seams are without seam allowances
- at the back-shoulder the fullness of 0.75 cm is kept short
- for more information on the shoulder seam and the **shoulder pad** see also page 92.

Inclination of side-part (Page 60)
- the amount for the inclination of the side part results from the body shape of the customer: normal 1.5 cm, strong 2 cm, with belly 2.5 cm

Taken measurements

	1/2	1/4	1/8	1/16
Height (*HEI*)	180	90	45	22.5	11.25
Chest (*CHE*)	108	54	27	13.5	
Waist (*WAI*)	94	47	23.5		
Hip (*HIP*)	108	54	27		
Neck (*NE*)	42				

Calculated measurements

Depth of syce (*DOS*)	= 1/16 *HEI* + 1/8 *CHE* = 24.75 cm
Waist length (*WL*)	= 1/4 *HEI* = 45 cm
Depth of hips (*DOH*)	= 1/8 *HEI* = 22.5 cm
Length (*LG*)	= 1/8 *HEI* x 3.5 = 78.75 ~ 79 cm
Neckline (*NL*)	= 1/6 *NE* + 1.5 = 8.5 cm
Back width (*BW*)	more than 100 chest =1/10 *CHE* +10.5 =21.3 ~ 21.5 cm
	less than 100 chest 2/10 *CHE* + 0.5
Width of scye (*WOS*)	= 1/8 *CHE* + 2.5 = 16 cm
Chest width (*CW*)	= 2/10 *CHE* + 2 = 23.6 ~ 23.5 cm
Front waist length (*FWL*)	upright posture *DOS* + 4 cm
	normal posture *DOS* + 3.5 = 28.25 ~ 28.5 cm
	stooped posture *DOS* + 3 cm

Double-breasted jacket
Follow the instructions for the single-breasted jacket to picture 1 on page 62 and continue on page 79. The front edge is used as a grainline reference; in case of stripes or a check, the darts should be laid straight in line with the cloth pattern.

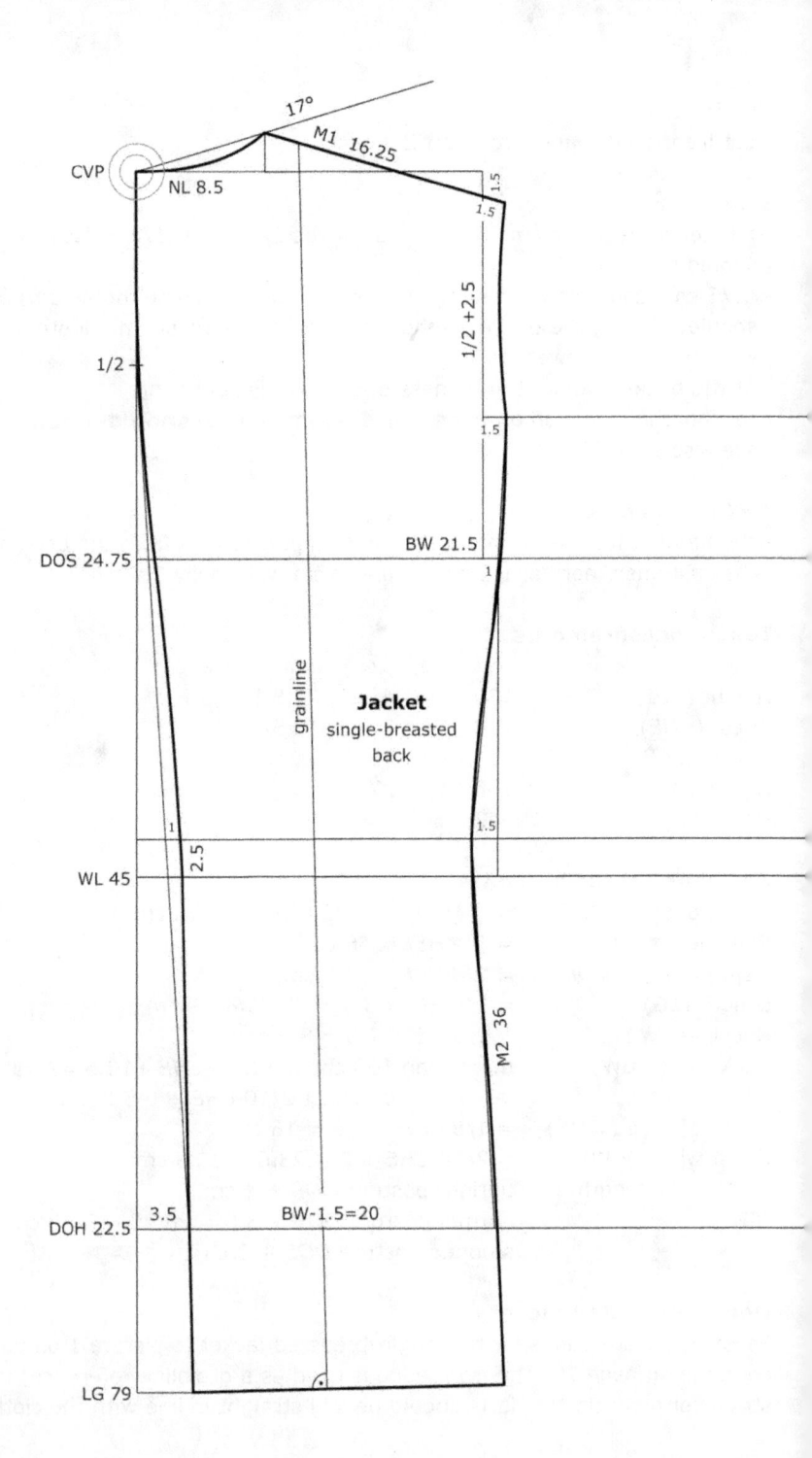

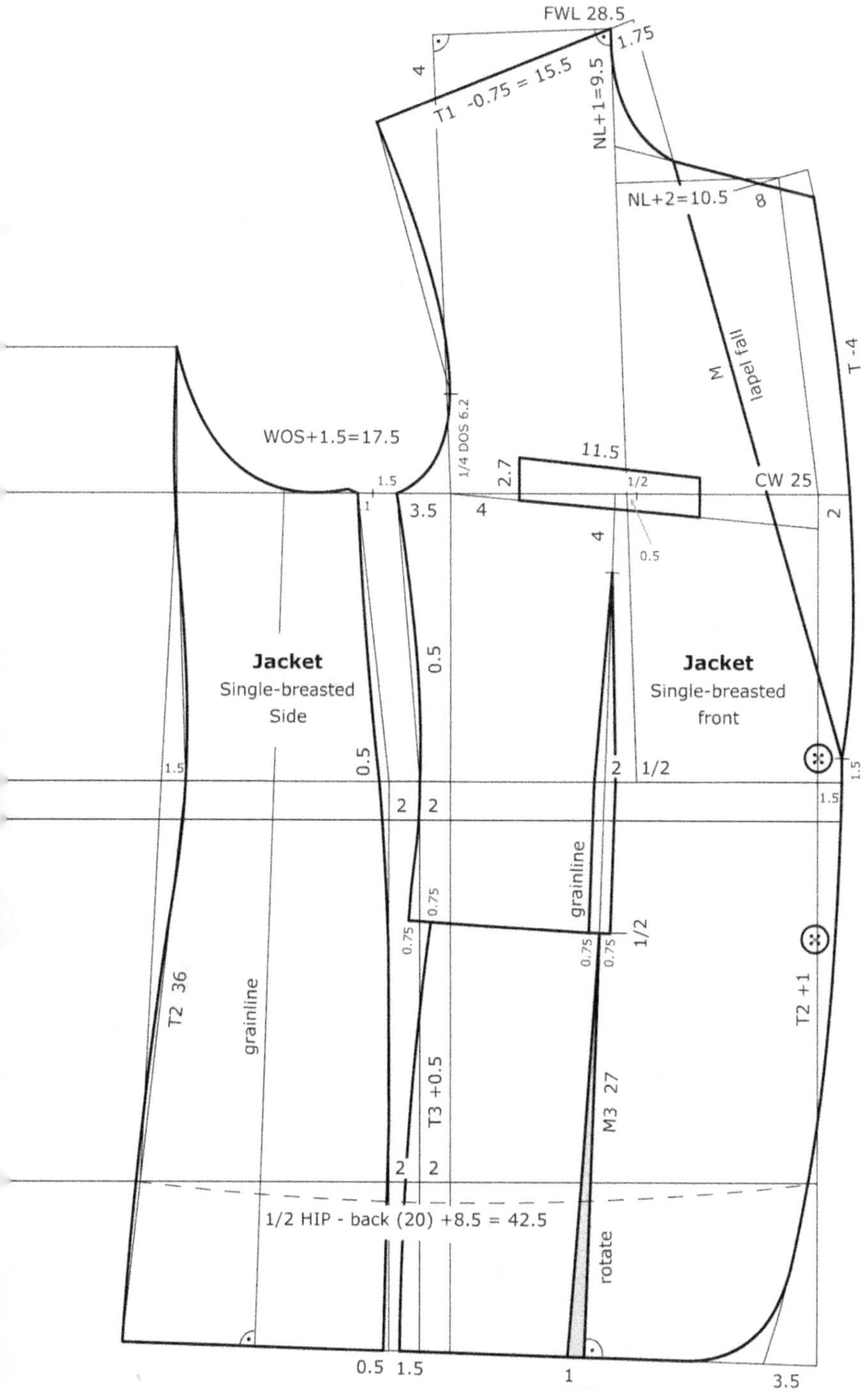
FWL 28.5
1.75
4
T1 -0.75 = 15.5
NL+1=9.5
NL+2=10.5
8
T -4
M
lapel fall
WOS+1.5=17.5
1/4 DOS 6.2
11.5
2.7
1/2
CW 25
1.5
1
3.5
4
2
4
0.5
Jacket
Single-breasted
Side
Jacket
Single-breasted
front
0.5
0.5
2
1/2
1.5
1.5
1.5
2
2
grainline
0.75
0.75
0.75
0.75
1/2
T2 36
grainline
T2 +1
T3 +0.5
M3 27
2
2
1/2 HIP - back (20) +8.5 = 42.5
rotate
0.5
1.5
1
3.5

Seam allowances

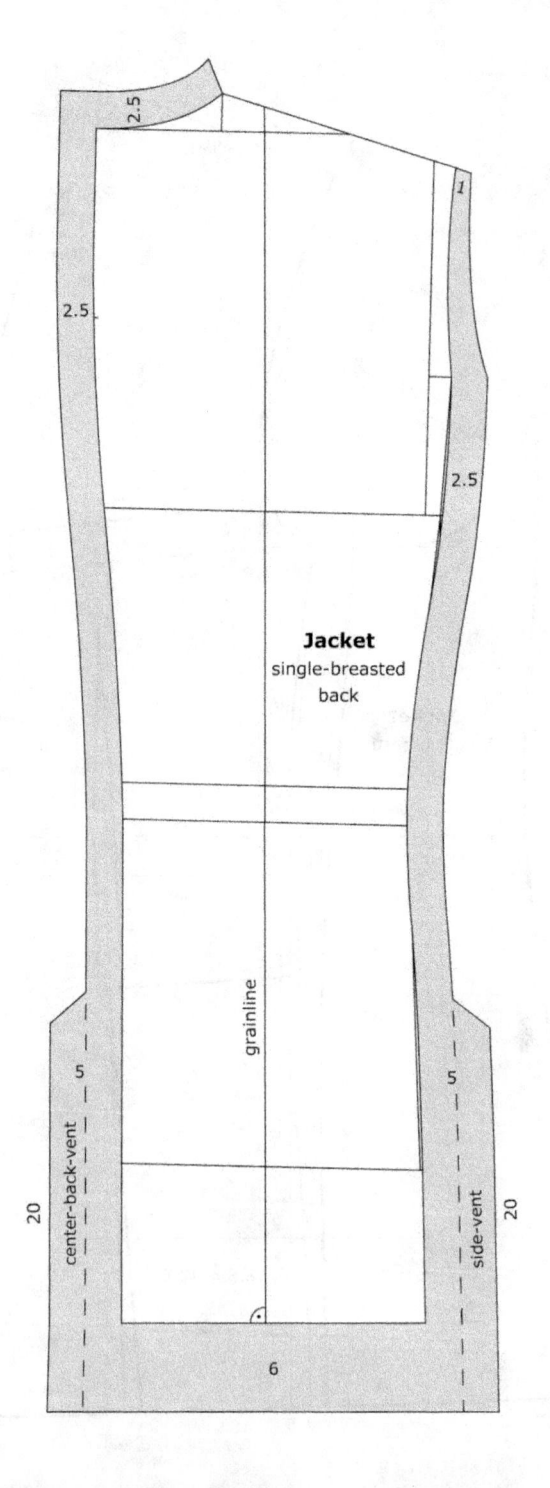

Jacket
single-breasted back

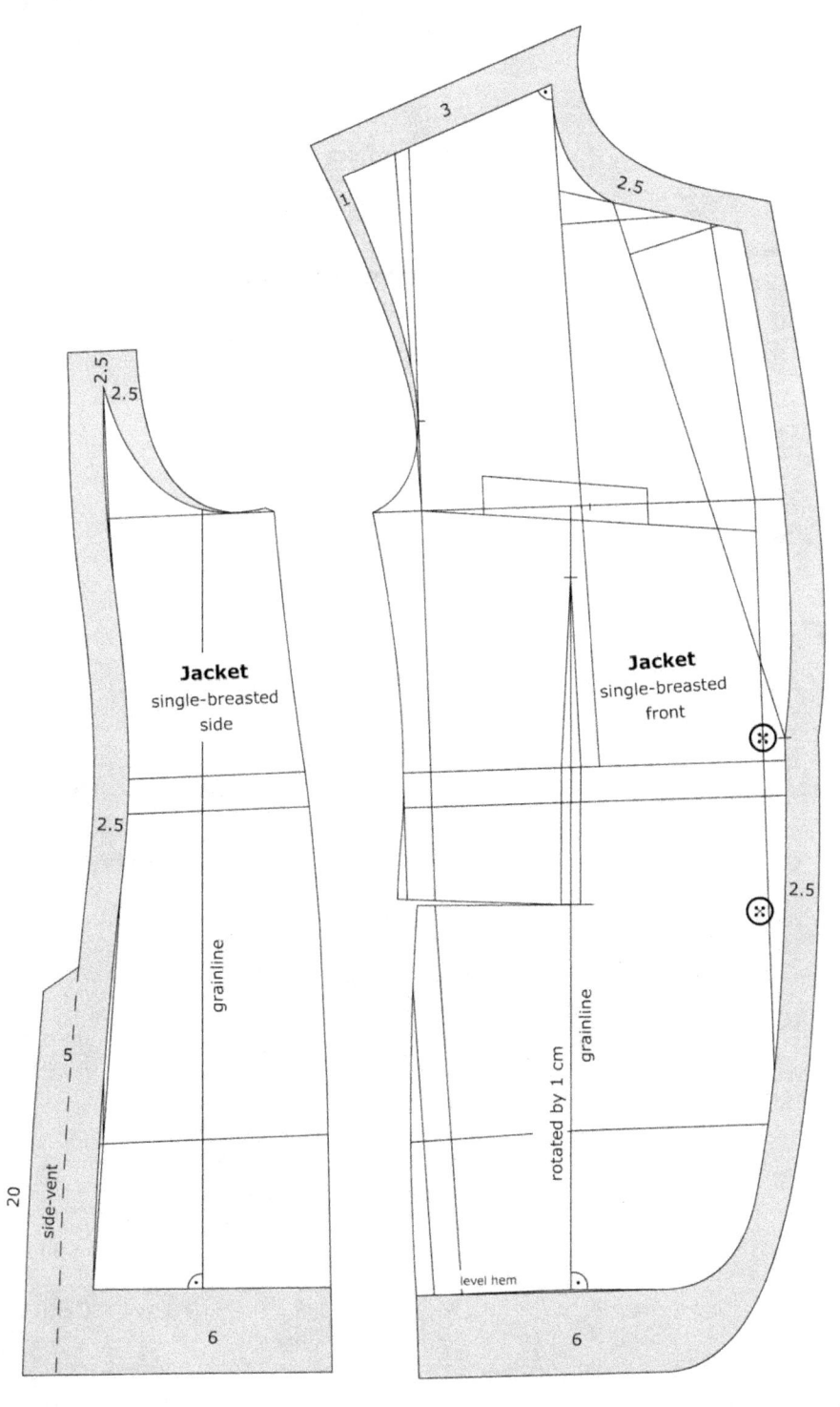

Manual for the jacket sleeve

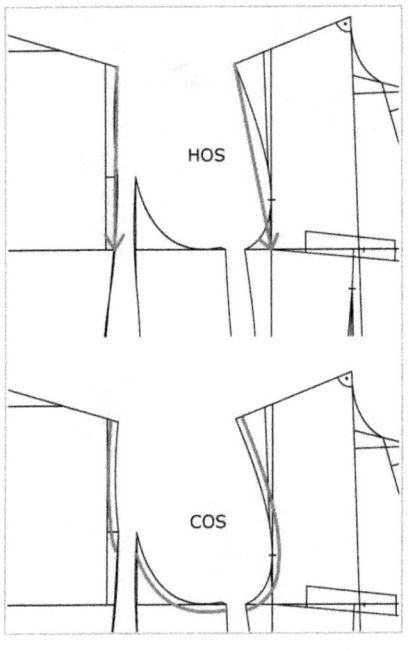

Height of scye
- measure front and back height-of-scye *HOS* and add up = 46.5 cm

Cirfumference of Scye
- measure circumference-of-scye *COS* minus seam allowances 3 cm = 54 cm (front and back-shoulder as well as front and back side-part-seam = 4 seams = 4 x 0.75 = 3 cm)

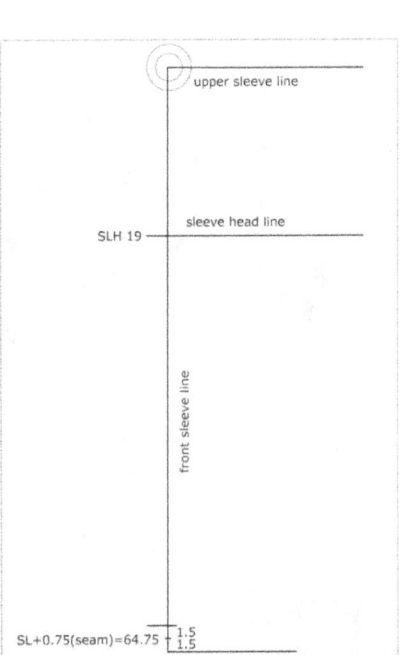

Start
- draw right angle
- vertical line defines the front-sleeve-line
- horizontal line defines the upper-sleeve-line

Basic frame
- at front-sleeve-line from upper-sleeve-line: mark down sleeve-head *SLH* = 1/2 *HOS* - (1/20 *HOS* + 2) = 19 cm and square right and left
- this defines the sleeve-head-line
- from upper-sleeve-line: mark down sleeve-length *SL* + 0.75 cm (seam allowance) = 64.75 cm
- from sleeve-lenght: mark up 1.5 cm and square left
- from sleeve-lenght: mark down 1.5 cm and square right

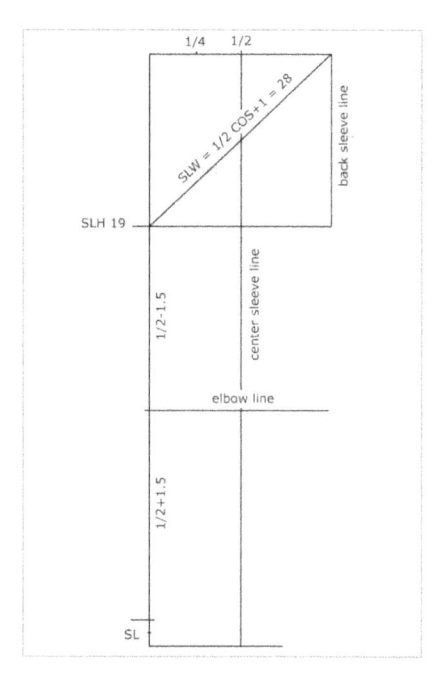

Sleeve width
- at front-sleeve-line from *SLH:* draw up diagonal touching the upper-sleeve-line, sleeve-width $SLW = 1/2\ COS + 1 = 28$ cm
- square down from previous point at upper-sleeve-line
- this defines the back-sleeve-line
- halve upper-sleeve-line and square down
- this defines the sleeve-center-line and also the grain-line
- halve the front part of the upper-sleeve-line

Elbow-line
- at front-sleeve-line: halve the distance between *SL* und *SLH*, mark down 1.5 cm and square right
- this defines the elbow-line

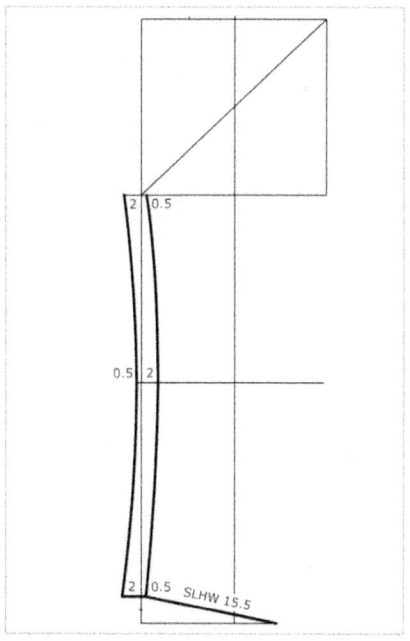

Front sleeve seam
- at *SL* from front-sleeve-line: mark to the left 2 cm and to the right 0.5 cm
- on elbow-line from front-sleeve-line: mark to the left 0.5 cm and to the right 2 cm
- on sleeve-head-line from front-sleeve-line: mark to the left 2 cm and to the right 0.5 cm
- connect all points with a curved line as shown

Sleeve hem width
- at *SL* from front-sleeve-line: mark down diagonal sleeve-hem-width *SLHW* 15.5 cm, touching the lower line as shown

The jacket sleeve

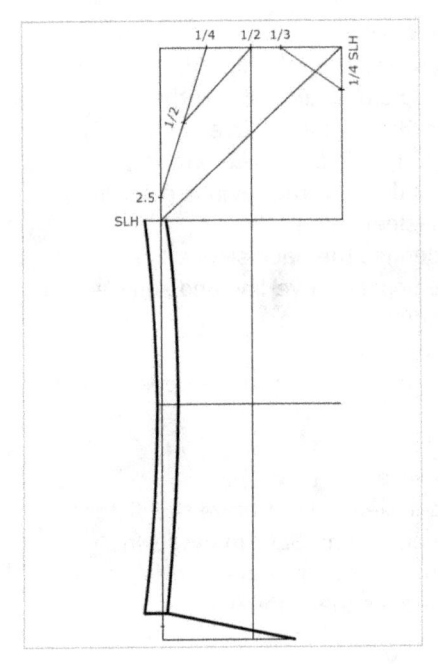

Sleeve head
- at front-sleeve-line from *SLH*:
  mark up 2.5 cm
- from this point mark up diagonal to first point on upper-sleeve-line
- halve this line and connect this point with second point on upper-sleeve-line

- divide the back part of the upper-sleeve-line into three
- on back-sleeve-line from upper-sleeve-line: mark down 1/4 *SLH* = 4.75 cm
- connect this point with 1/3 point on upper-sleeve-line
- see also bigger pattern drawing on page 75

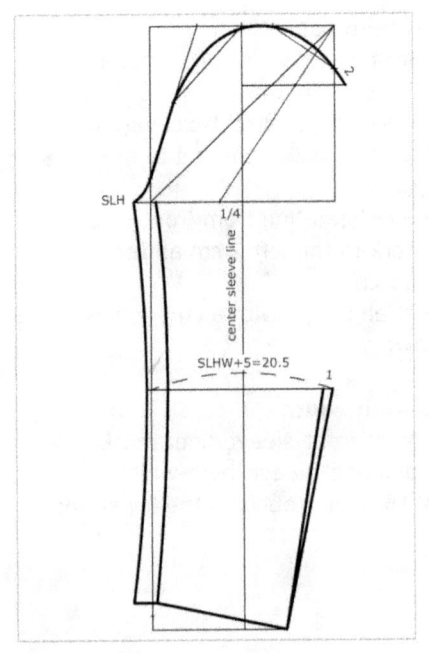

Upper sleeve
- shape sleeve head as shown
- extend back part of sleeve-head by 2 cm
- square left as shown

Undersleeve
- on elbow-line from front-sleeve-line: mark to the right sleeve-hem-width *SLHW* + 5 = 20.5 cm
- from this point mark to the left 1 cm
- draw lines to point on lower line as shown

- on *SLH*-line from sleeve-center-line: divide the distance into four
- connect this point with right point on upper-sleeve-line

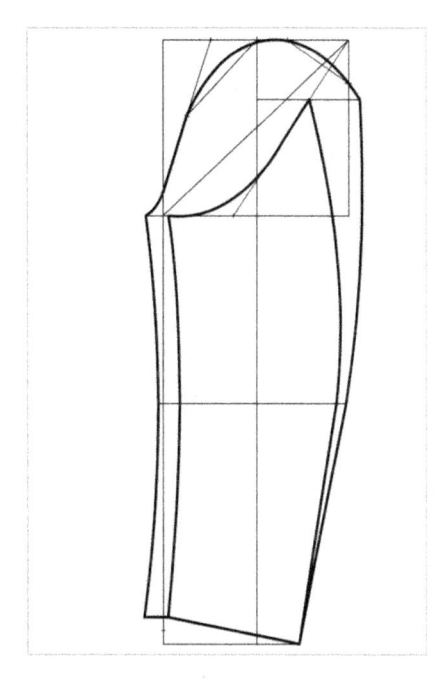

Finish Sleeve
- draw back-seam with a curved line
- finish undersleeve as shown on page 75
- copy undersleeve as a separate pattern piece
- the fullness in the sleeve-head is approx. 3.5 cm

Sleeve notches
In the pattern consciously no sleeve-notch was defined on the sleeve, because the arm level is different for each person.

Create notch
The sleeve is held on top of the sleeve-head and turned into the correct position. Then the position of the shoulder-seam is transfered to the sleeve-head.

Cutting
- cut upper sleeve 2 x
- cut undersleeve 2 x

Instructions
- back sleeve-seam and sleeve-hem are without seam-allowance
- all other seams are including 0.75 cm seam allowance (sewing machine foot width)
- the sleeve-center-line serves as a grainline reference

Measurements
Sleeve length (SL)	64
Circumference of scye (COS)	54 | 27
Heigth of scye (HOS)	46.5 | 23.25
Width of scye (WOS)	16 (measurement from the jacket or coat)
Sleeve head (SLH)	$1/2\ HOS - (1/20\ HOS + 2) = 18.95 \sim 19$ cm
Sleeve width (SLW)	$1/2\ COS + 1 = 28$ cm
Sleeve hem width ($SLHW$)	approx. 15.5 cm

Seam allowances

Jacket underslave

Jacket upper-sleeve

Jacket
undersleeve

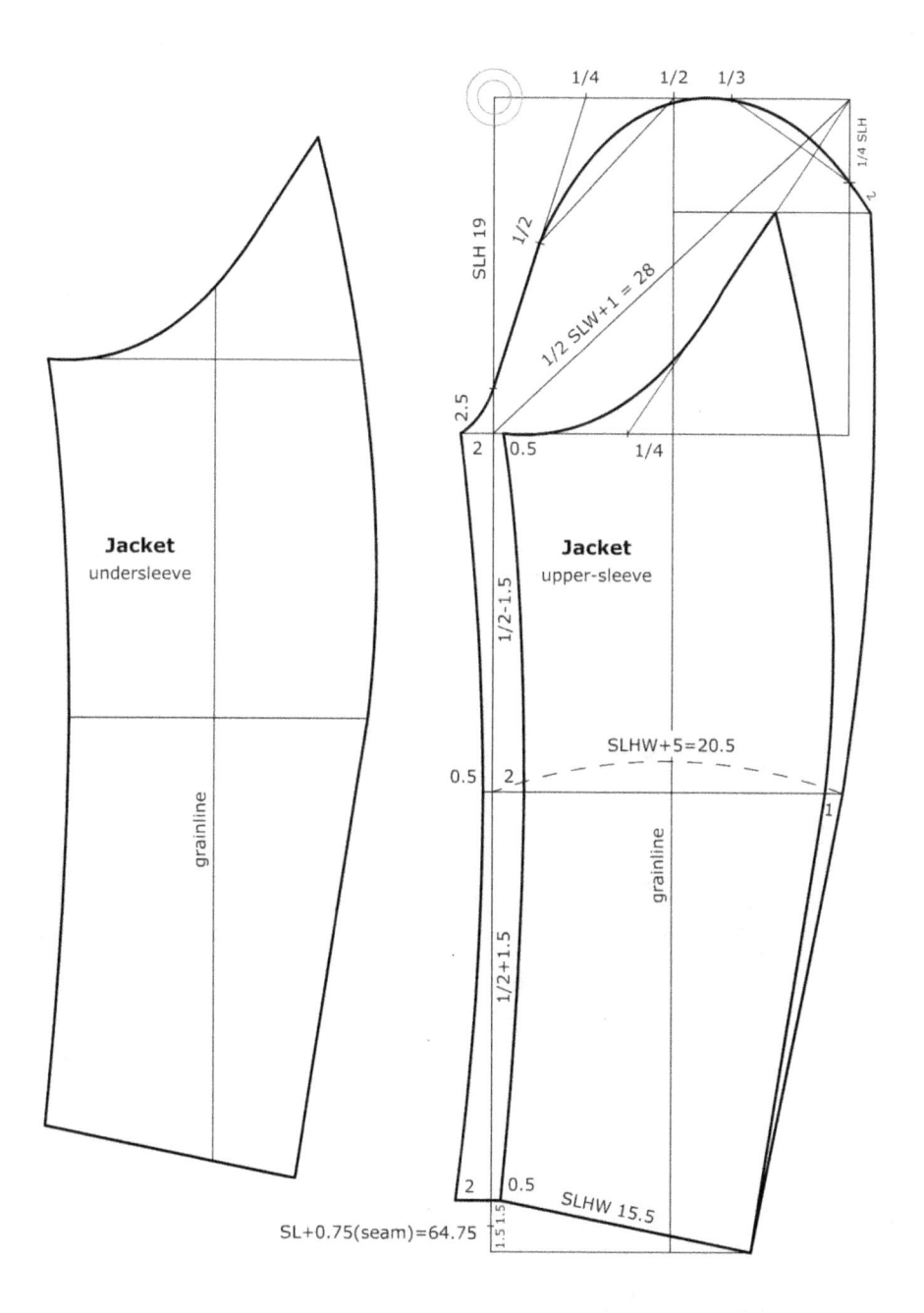

Jacket
upper-sleeve

1/4 1/2 1/3

SLH 19

1/4 SLH

1/2

1/2 SLW+1 = 28

2.5

2 0.5 1/4

1/2−1.5

SLHW+5=20.5

0.5 2

1

1/2+1.5

2 0.5 SLHW 15.5

1.5 1.5

SL+0.75(seam)=64.75

grainline

grainline

Manual for the single-breasted jacket collar

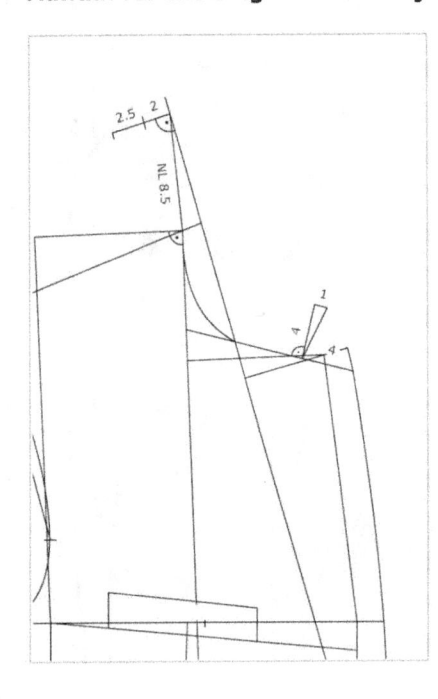

Start
- extend the line of the lapel-fall
- from tip of shoulder/neckline: mark up neckline NL = 8.5 cm touching the extended lapel-fall
- from this point: square to the left using the extended lapel-fall-line
- on this line: first mark to the left 2 cm and then mark 2.5 cm as shown

- from lapel-tip: mark to the left 4 cm and square up
- on this line mark up 4 cm, square left and mark 1 cm
- connect both points as shown

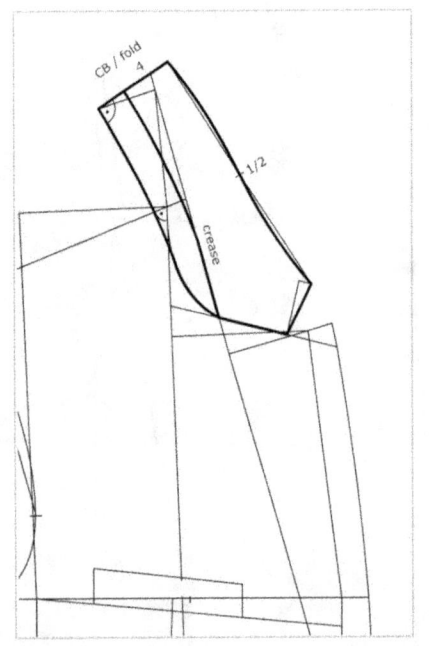

- draw curving line for neckline-seam
- draw curving line for collar-crease-line
- at center back CB/fold from neckline-seam: square right
- at CB from collar-crease-line: mark to the right 4 cm
- connect this point with point at collar-tip
- halve this line
- shape collar nicely as shown

Jacket
collar

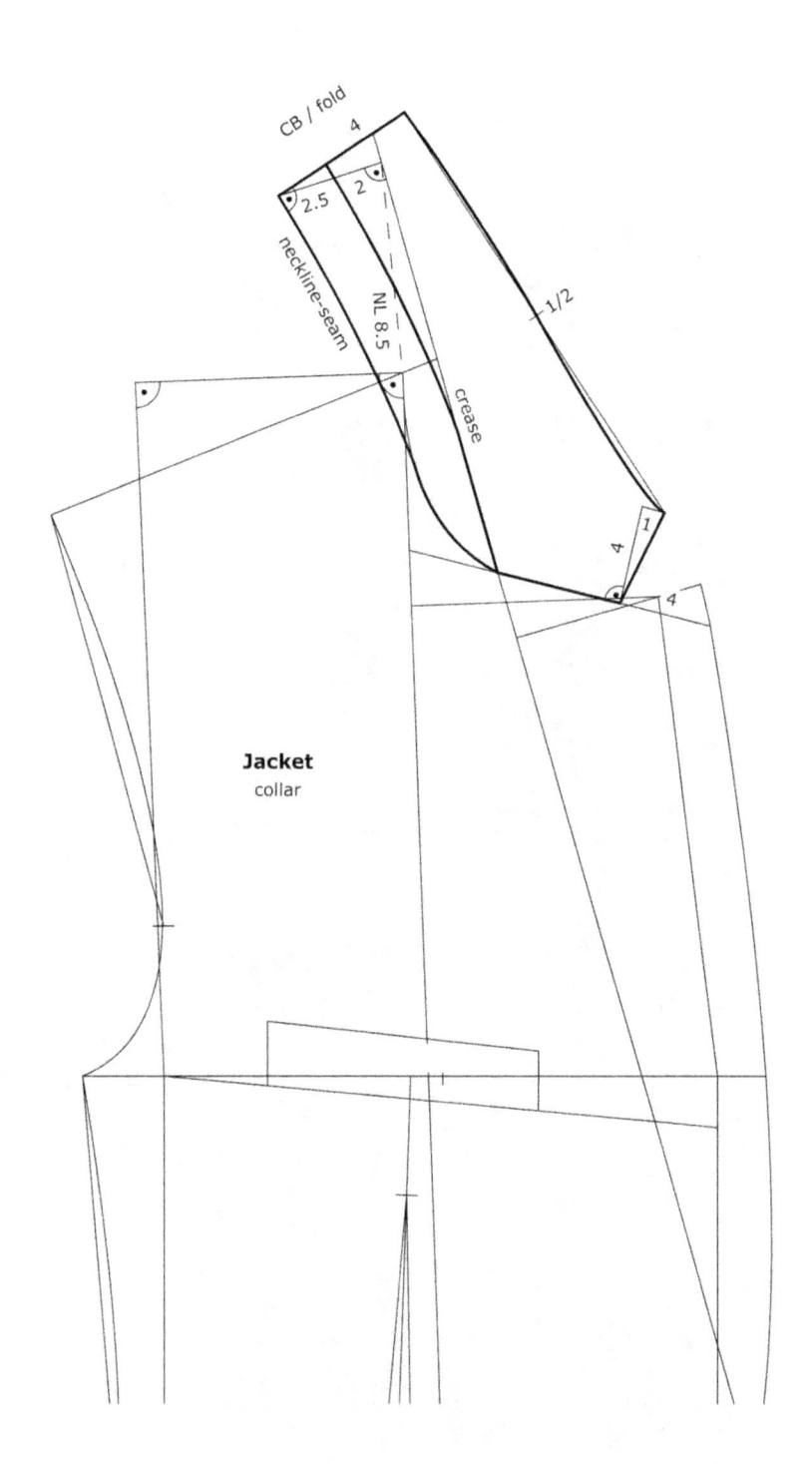

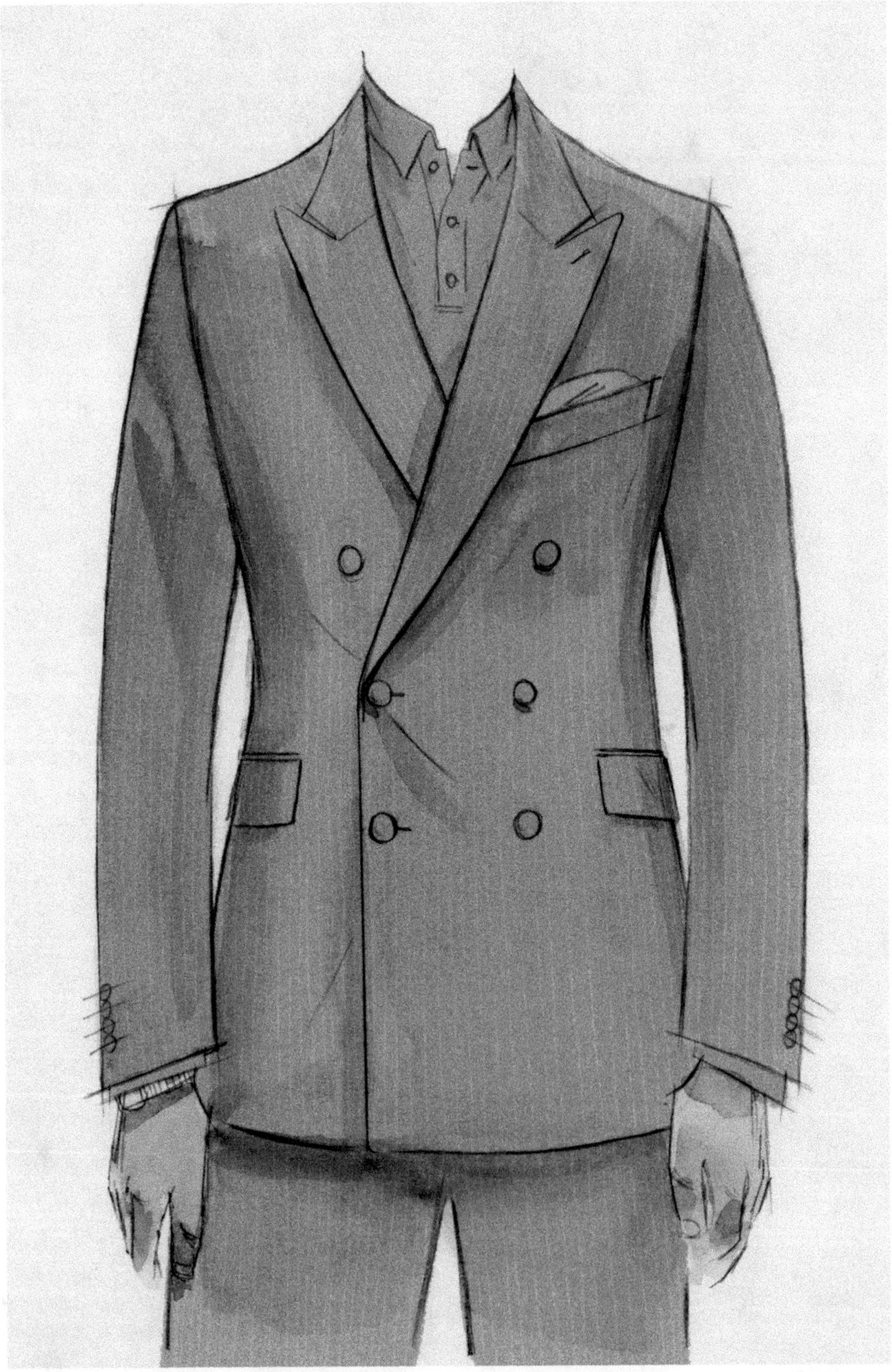

Manual for the double-breasted jacket

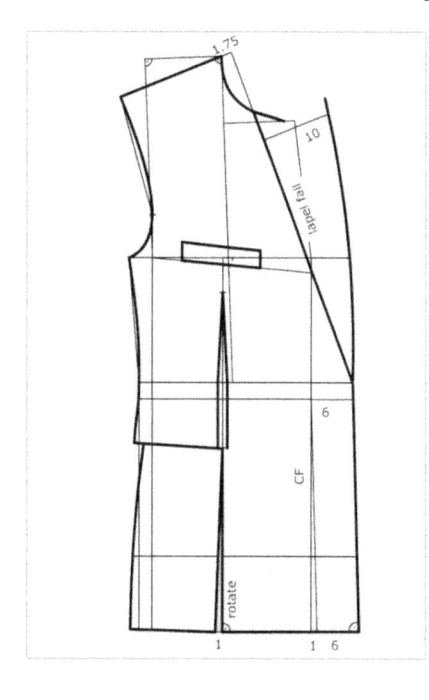

Lapel-fall
- extend shoulder-line to the right and mark 1.75 cm
- on elevated waist from center front *CF*: extend to the right 6 cm
- connect both points
- on lapel-fall: square right touching the tip of *CF*/neckline
- on this line: mark 10 cm for lapel-width
- draw curved line for lapel-edge

Front edge
- at *CF* on hem-line: mark to the right 1 cm and connect with *CF* at waist-line
- On hem-line from *CF*: mark to the right 6 cm and connect this point with point at elevated waist/front edge
- the lower front edge serves as the grainline

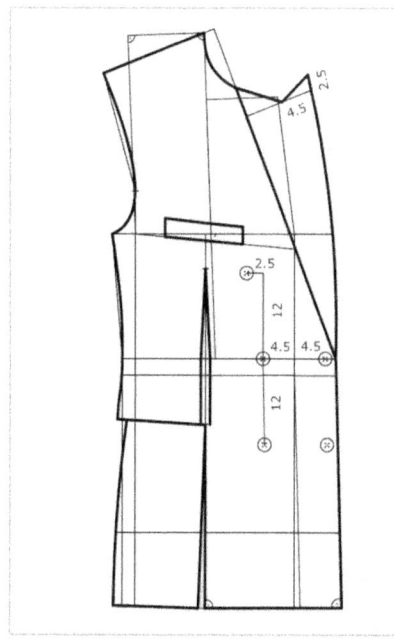

Lapel
- at lapel-edge: mark up 2.5 cm as shown
- at width-of-lapel-line: mark 4,5 cm
- connect both points
- shape neckline nicely

Buttons
- on elevated-waist-line from *CF*: mark to each side 4.5 cm
- from here mark down 12 cm for lower buttons
- the upper button will be placed 12 cm up and 2.5 cm to the left

Dart and pockets
- follow the instructions of the single-breasted jacket from page 63

79

Seam allowances

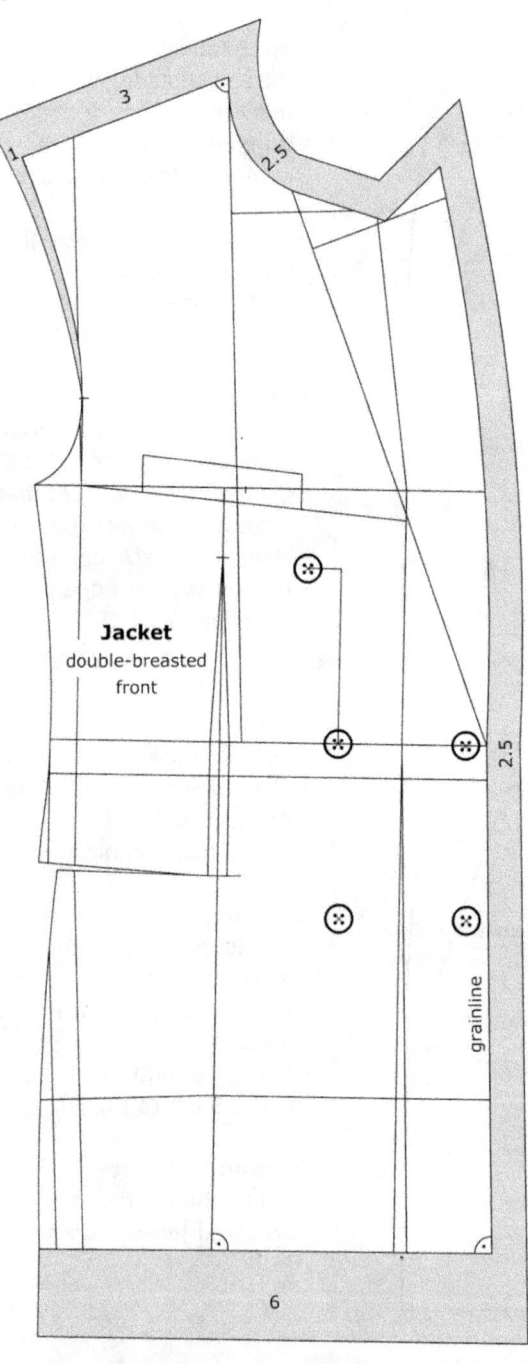

Jacket
double-breasted front

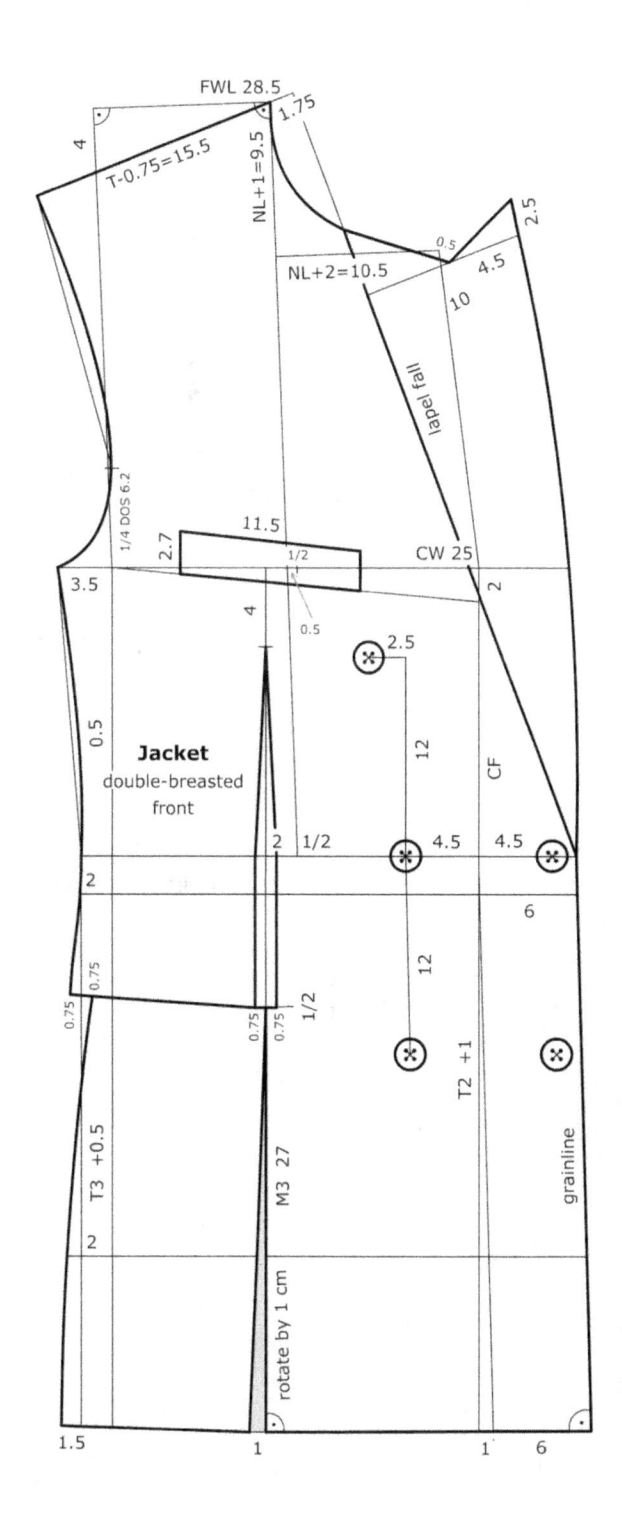

Jacket double-breasted front

Manual for the double-breasted jacket collar

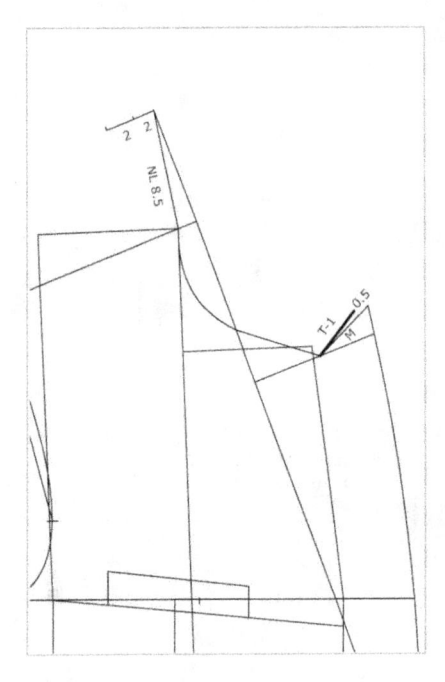

Start
- extend the line of the lapel-fall
- from tip of shoulder/neckline:
  mark up neckline NL = 8.5 cm touching the extended lapel-fall
- from this point: square left using the extended lapel-fall-line
- on this line: first mark 2 cm and then mark 2 cm again as shown

- at collar-tip: draw diagonal line with a 0.5 cm gap to the lapel-tip
  (see also page 83)
- at lapel-tip: measure distance M = 5.5 cm and tranfer to the collar-tip
  $T - 1$ = 4.5 cm

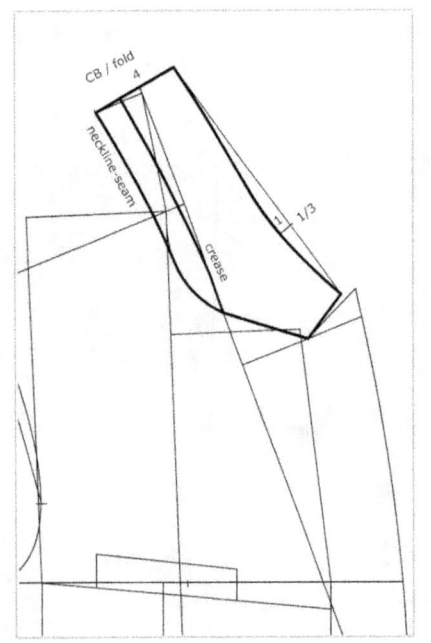

- draw curving line for neckline-seam
- draw curving line for collar-crease-line
- at center back CB/fold from neckline-seam: square right
- at CB from collar-crease-line: mark to the right 4 cm
- connect this point with point at collar-tip
- divide this line into three, square left and mark 1 cm
- shape collar nicely

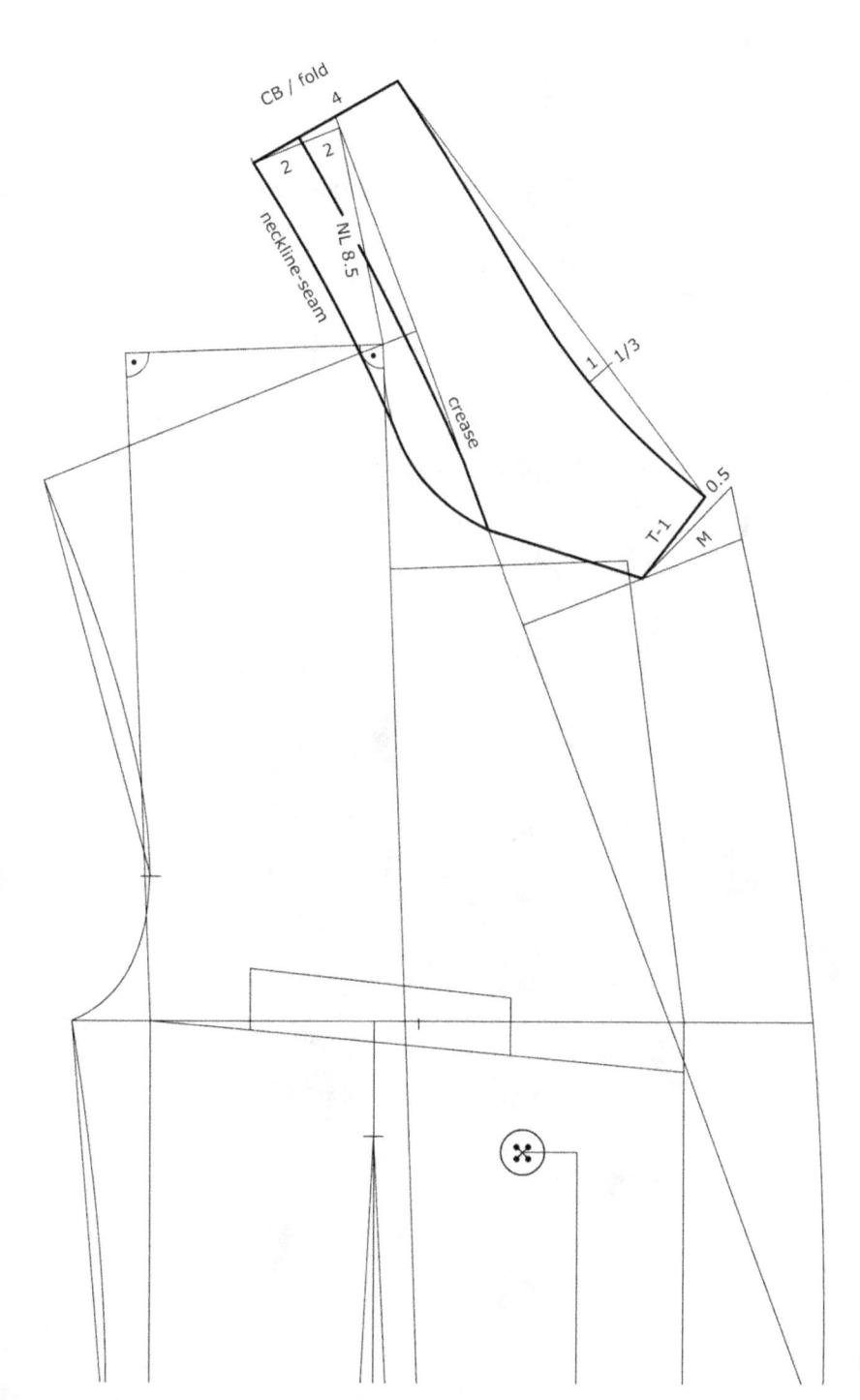

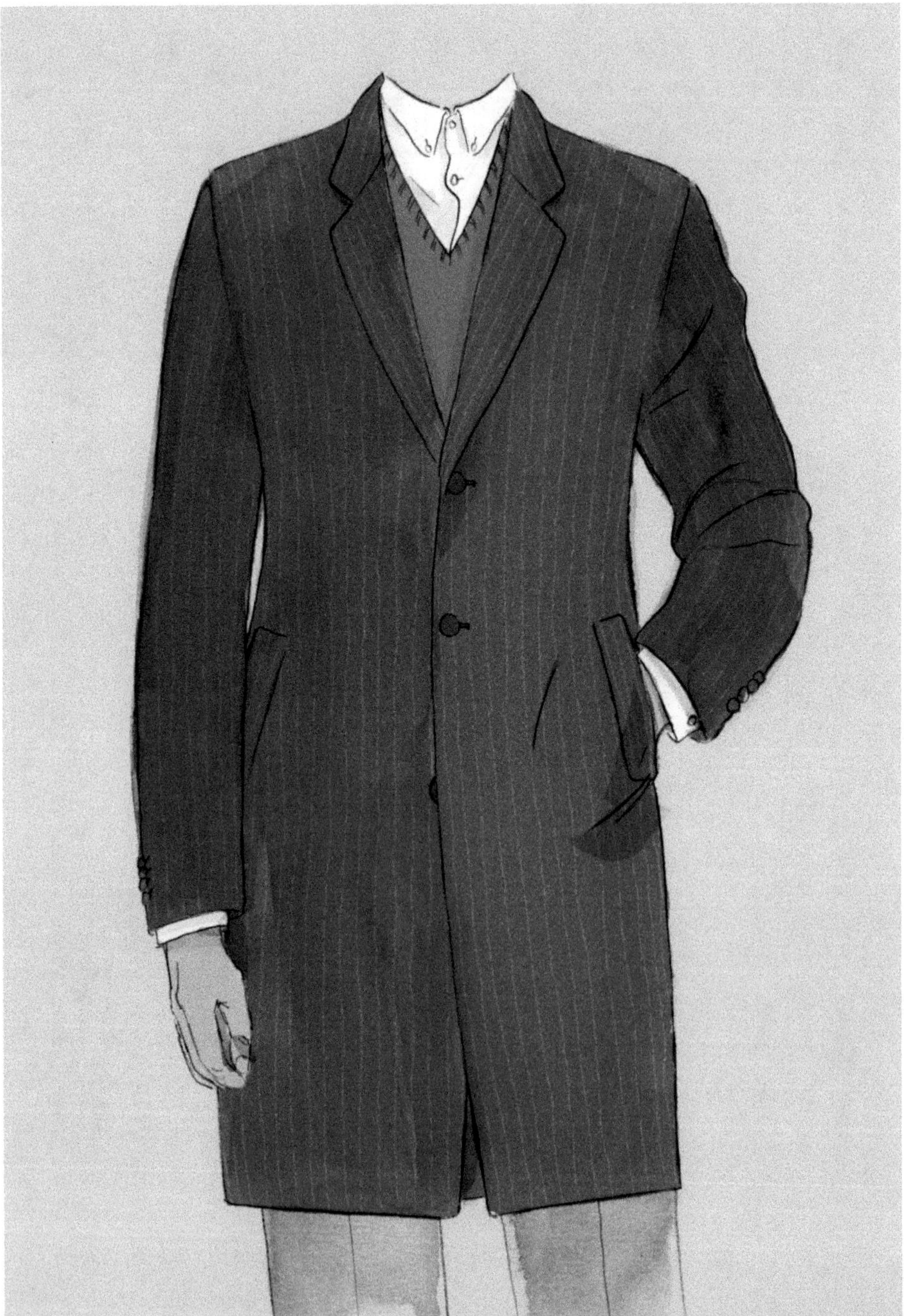

Manual for the single-breasted coat

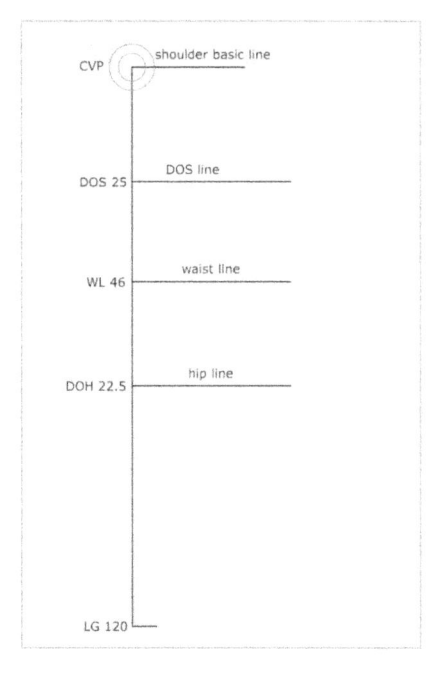

Start
- draw right angle
- vertical line is the center-back-basic-line
- horizontal line is the basic-shoulder-line
- at center-back-basic-line from the 7th cervical-vertebra-point *CVP*: mark down *DOS* = 1/16 *HEI* + 1/8 *CHE* = 25 cm and square right
- at center-back-basic-line from *CVP*: mark down waist-length *WL* = 1/4 *HEI* + 1 = 46 cm and square right
- at center-back-basic-line from *WL*: mark down *DOH* = 1/8 *HEI* = 22.5 cm and square right
- at center-back-basic-line from *CVP*: mark down length *LG* = 1/2 *HEI* + approx. 30 = 120 cm and square right

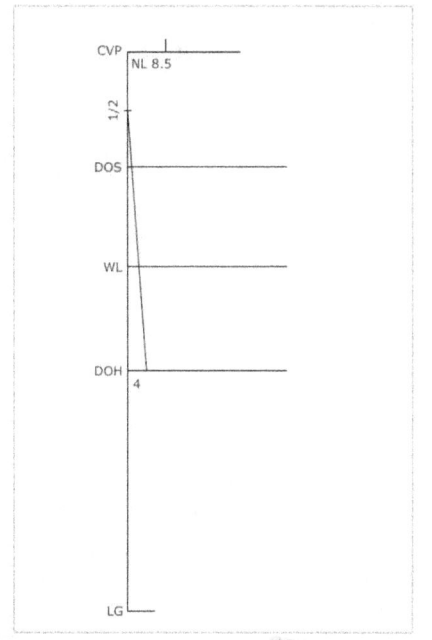

Back seam
- on center-back-basic-line: halve the distance between *CVP* and *WL*
- at *Hip*-line from center-back-basic-line: mark to the right 4 cm and connect this point with previous point

Neck/Shoulder
- at shoulder-basic-line from *CVP*: mark to the right neckline *NL* = 1/6 *NE* + 1.5 = 8.5 cm and square up

85

The single-breasted coat

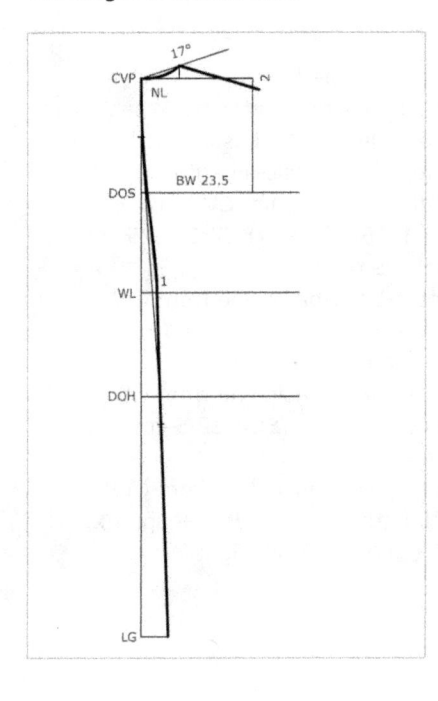

Back seam
- on *WL*-line: mark to the right 1 cm as shown
- from this point: draw down line through point at *HIP*-line
- shape back-seam nicely

Shoulder
- on *DOS*-line from *CB*: mark to the right back-width $BW = 1/10\ CHE + 12.5 = 23.5$ cm and square up (attention: see also calculation of *BW* on page 93)
- from *CVP*: create 17° angle to the right up
- from shoulder-basic-line at *BW*-line: mark down 2 cm and connect with upper point at the neckline

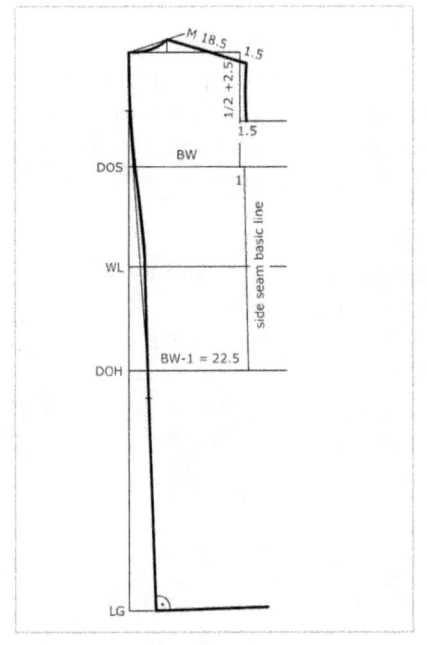

Scye/Armhole
- at shoulder from *BW*-line: extend shoulder-seam to the right by 1.5 cm and measure $M = 18.5$ cm (you will need this later for the front shoulder)
- on *BW*-line from shoulder: mark down half the distance + 2.5 cm, square right and mark 1.5 cm
- shape back-armhole nicely

Preperation for side seam
- on *DOS*-line from *BW*-line: mark to the right 1 cm (to hide the side seam under the sleeve
- on *HIP*-line from *CB*: mark to the right $BW - 1 = 22.5$ cm
- connect this point with previous point, this defines the side-seam-basic-line
- at *Lg* from *CB*: square to the right

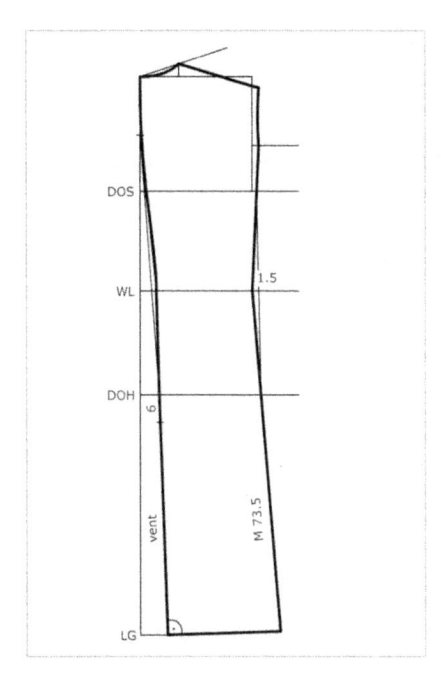

Sideseam
- on waist-line from side-seam-basic-line: mark to the left 1.5 cm
- from this point: draw straight line through point at *HIP*-line
- shape side seam nicely
- on side seam from waist: measure down *M* to *LG* = 73.5 cm (you will need this for the sideseam)

Vent at CB
- at back-seam from *HIP*-line: mark down 6 cm

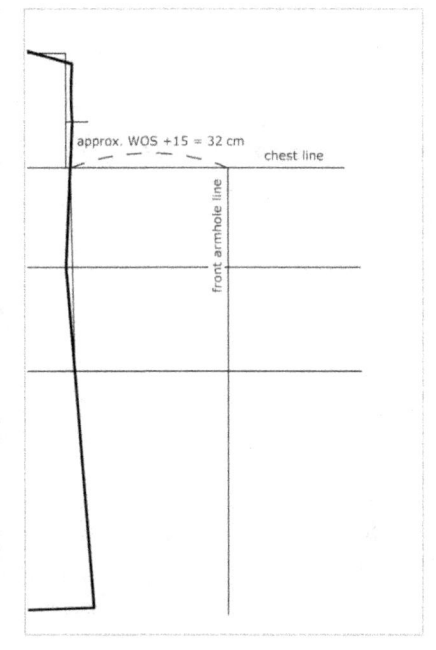

Extend lines for front piece
- extend chest-line (also known as *DOS*-line), waist-line, and hip-line to the right
- on chest-line: mark to the right *WOS* + approx. 15 = 32 cm and square down (the 15 cm are chosen at random to get enaugh space to the back)
- this line defines the front-armhole-line

The single-breasted coat

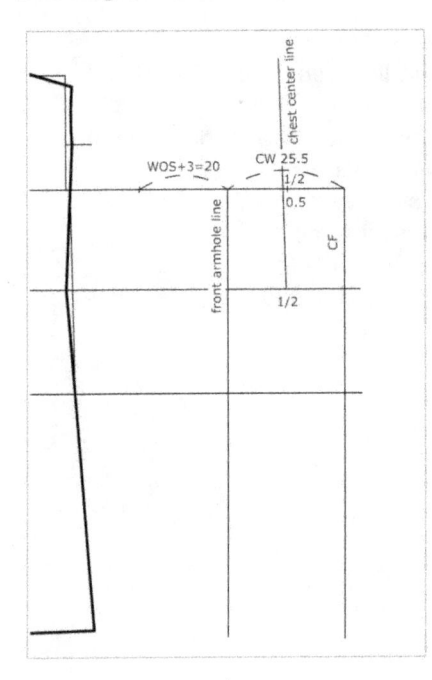

Width of scye
- on chest-line from front-armhole-line: mark to the left
  $WOS = 1/8\ CHE + 3.5 = 17$ cm $+ 3$
  (**for the inclination of the side part**, see page 92) $= 20$ cm

Chest width
- on chest-line from front-armhole-line: mark to the right, chest width
  $CW = 2/10\ CHE + 4 = 25.5$ cm
  and square down
- this line defines the center-front CF
- halve CW and mark to the left 0.5 cm
- halve distance at waist-line
- connect both points as shown
- this line defines the center-chest-line

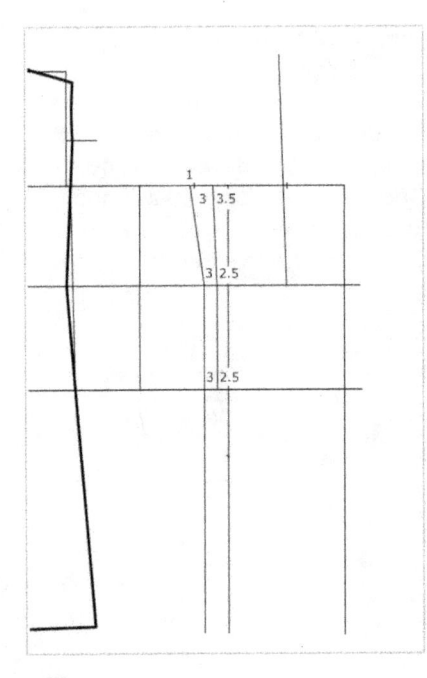

Side piece
- on chest-line form front-armhole-line: mark to the left 3.5 cm
- from this point mark to the left 3 cm for **the inclination of the side part** (see eplanation on page 92)
- and from this point: mark to the left 1 cm (the amount from the displaced back-seam)

- on waist-line from front-armhole-line: mark to the left 2.5 cm
- from this point: mark to the left 3 cm

- on hip-line from front-armhole-line: mark to the left 2.5 cm
- from this point mark to the left 3 cm
- connect all points as shown

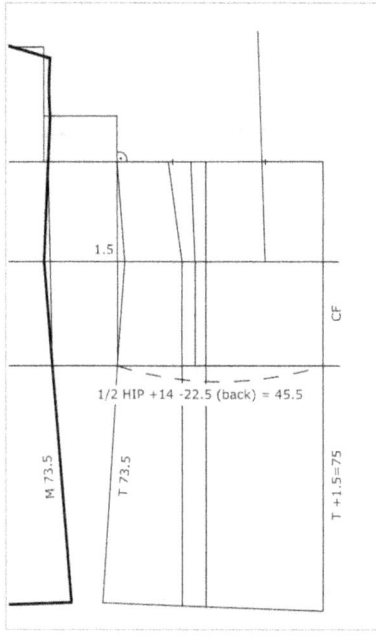

Sideseam
- on hip-line from *CF*: mark to the left
  1/2 *HIP* - 22.5 cm (width of lower back)
  + 14 (fullness and space between front-
  and side-part) = 45.5 cm
- connect this point with *WOS*-point on
  chest-line

- on waist-line: mark to the right 1.5 cm
  and draw side seam
- on chest-line from side seam: square up
  to the line coming from the back part

- at back sideseam from waist: measure
  distance to length *M* = approx. 73.5 cm
  and tranfer to front side seam
  T = 73.5 cm
- at *CF* from waist-line: mark down this
  distance + 1.5 = 75 cm
- connect both points at length

Front armhole
- on chest-line from center-chest-line:
  mark up front-shoulder *FWL* = *DOS* + 3.5
  = approx. 28.5 cm
  (see also calculation on page 92)
- from this point square left
- from this line: square down to crossing
  point of chest-line and front-armhole-line
- on this line from chest-line: mark up
  1/4 *DOS* = 6.2 cm

Shoulder
- at front-armhole-line from top:
  mark down 4 cm
- draw shoulder-seam and transfer length
  of back-shoulder-seam - 1 cm = 17.5 cm
- shape front armhole nicely

The single-breasted coat

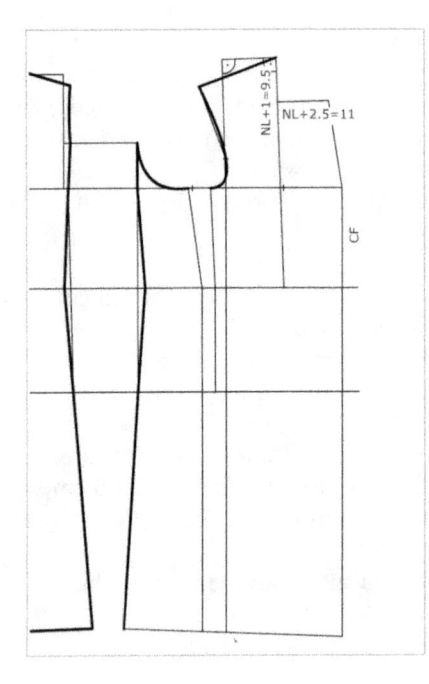

Side part armhole
- shape armhole of side part nicely

Sideseam
- shape sideseam nicely
- side seam is without any seam allowance

Neckline
- on center-line from shoulder: mark down neckline $NL + 1 = 9.5$ cm, square right and mark $NL + 2.5 = 11$ cm
- connect this point with CF on chest-line

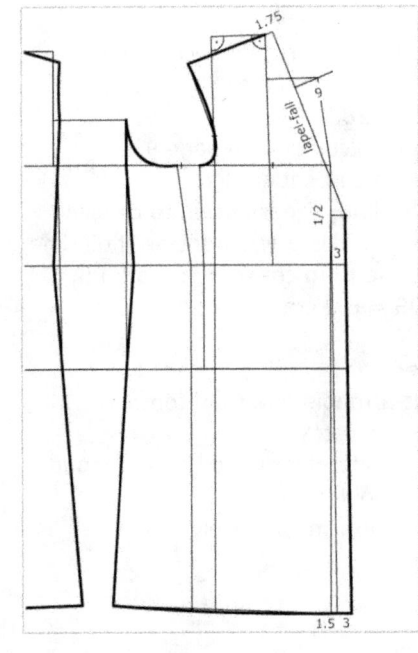

Lapel fall
- extend shoulder-line to the right and mark 1.75 cm
- at CF: halve distance between chest-line and waist-line and square right
- on this line: mark 3 cm
- connect this point with previous point at shoulder-line
- on lapel-fall: square to the right to tip of CF/neckline
- on this line mark 9 cm for lapel-width

Front edge
- on hem-line from CF: mark to the left 1.5 cm and dislocate center-front a little forward
- on hem-line from new CF: mark to the right 3 cm for front edge
- shape hem sligthly curved

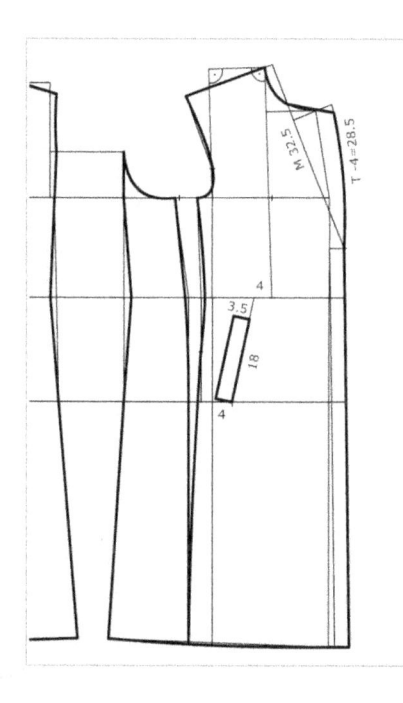

Neckline
- shape front neckline nicely

Lapel
- shape edge of lapel with a slight curve
- measure lapel-fall M = 32.5 cm and transfer T this measure - 4 = 28.5 cm to lapel-front-edge
- from lapel tip at CF: draw line to top of lapel-fall

Pocket
- on waist-line from center-line: mark to the left 4 cm
- on hip-line from front-armhole-line: mark to the right 4 cm
- connect both points
- mark pocket length with 18 cm
- mark width of welt pocket with 3.5 cm

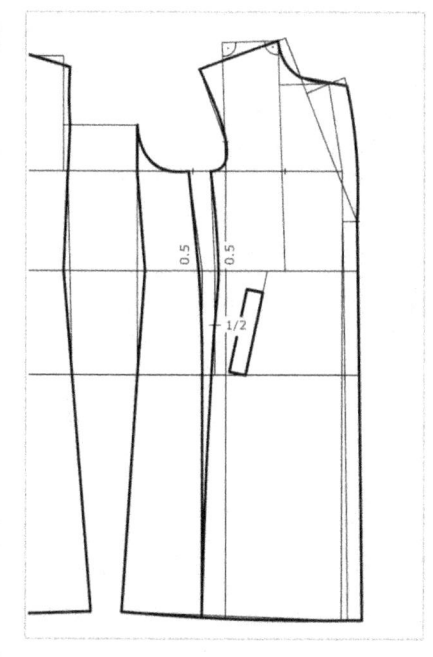

Side-part-seam
- at front side-part-seam from waist-line: draw down slightly curved line wich is touching the side-part at the hem

Narrow waist
- at side-part-seam: mark approx. 0.5 cm to each side (see also page 95)
- shape side-part-seam as shown

The single-breasted coat

Cutting
- cut front 2 x
- cut side 2 x
- cut back 2 x

Instructions
- all measures are in cm
- 0.75 cm seam allowances are included (sewing machine foot width) at the shoulder, the entire armhole and the side-part-seam, all other seams are without seam allowances
- at the back shoulder the fullness of 0.75 cm is kept short

Shoulder pads
Each shoulder is different and each customer wants a different shoulder line. Therefore, the thickness of the shoulder pads and the inclination and position of the shoulder seam are adjusted at the first fitting.

The inclination of the side-part (Page 88)
- the amount for tilting the side-part results from the body shape of the customer: normal about 3 cm, strong about 3.5 cm, with belly about 4 cm

Sleeve
- the pattern is made after measuring the height-of-scye and circumference-of-scye like the jacket sleeve (see page 70).
- the sleeve length of the coat can be 1.5 cm longer than the jacket sleeve.

Measured circumference-of-scye COS = 55 cm
Measured height-of-scye HOS = 46.5 cm

Collar
- the pattern of the collar for coats is like the collar of the jacket

Double breasted coat
Follow the instructions for the single-breasted coat as shown in picture 1 on page 90, then continue at page 97.

Control
Compare the width of chest, waist and hips of the pattern with the taken measurements. The fullness for each should be about 7.5 cm on the half, so about 15 cm on the entire width.

Taken measurements

	1/2	1/4	1/8	1/16
Height (*HEI*)	180	90	45	22.5	11.25
Chest (*CHE*)	108	54	27	13.5
Waist (*WAI*)	94	47	23.5
Hip (*HIP*)	108	54	27
Neck (*NE*)	42

Calculated measurements

Depth of scye (*DOS*) = 1/16 *HEI* + 1/8 *CHE* = 24.75 ~ 25 cm
Waist length (*WL*) = 1/4 *HEI* + 1 = 46 cm
Depth of hips (*DOH*) = 1/8 *HEI* = 22.5 cm
Length (*LG*) = 1/2 *HEI* + 30 = 120 cm
Neckline (*NL*) = 1/6 *NE* + 1.5 = 8.5 cm

Back width (*BW*)   more than 100 cm chest = 1/10 *CHE* + 12.5
(for a coat with jacket underneath) = 23.3 ~ 23.5 cm
less than 100 cm Chest 2/10 *CHE* + 2.5
(for a coat with jacket underneath)

Width of scye (*WOS*) = 1/8 *Ow* + 3.5 (for a coat with jacket underneath)
= 17 cm

Chest width (*CW*) = 2/10 *Ow* + 4 (for a coat with jacket underneath)
= 25.6 ~ 25.5 cm

Front waist length (*FWL*)
upright posture: *DOS* + 4 cm
normale posture: *DOS* + 3.5 = 28.5 cm
stooped posture: *DOS* + 3 cm

No Jacket underneeth

If no jacket is worn under the coat, the back-width, the width-of-scye and the chest-width can be calculated as for a jacket.

Seam allowances

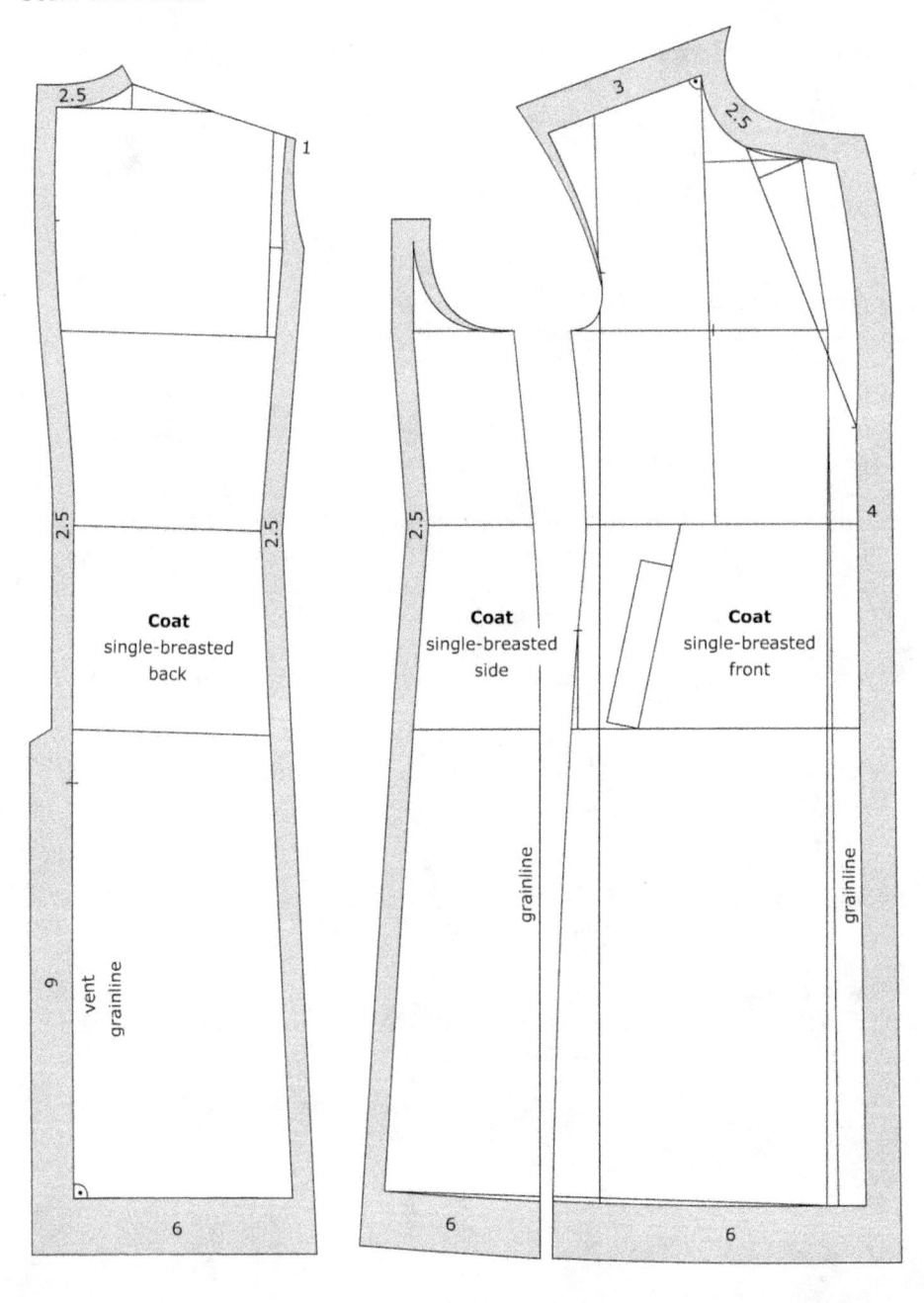

Coat
single-breasted
back

Coat
single-breasted
side

Coat
single-breasted
front

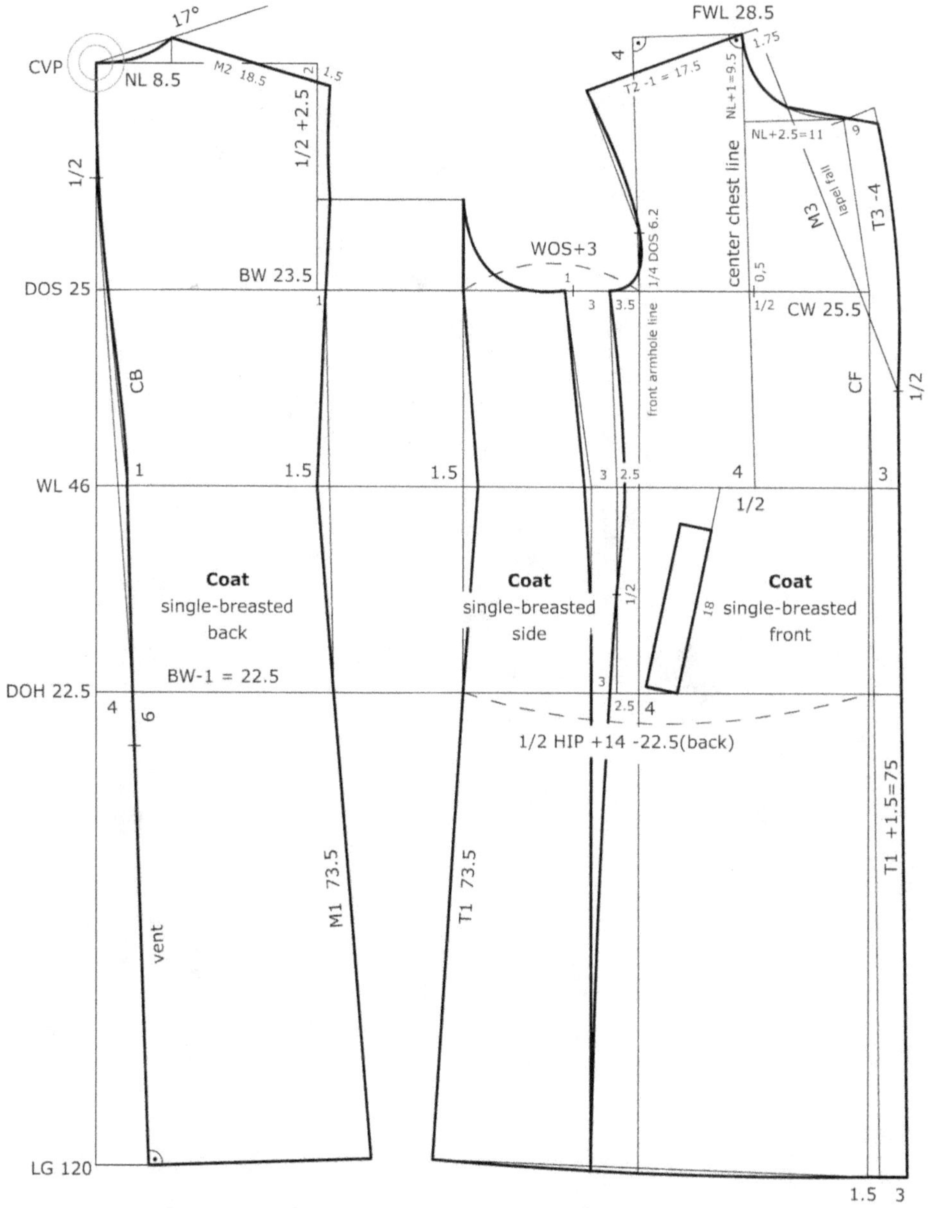

17°
CVP
NL 8.5
M2 18.5
2
1.5
1/2 +2.5
1/2
BW 23.5
DOS 25
1
CB
WL 46
1
1.5
1.5
Coat
single-breasted
back
BW-1 = 22.5
DOH 22.5
4
6
vent
M1 73.5
T1 73.5
LG 120
WOS+3
1
3
3.5
Coat
single-breasted
side
1/2 HIP +14 -22.5(back)
FWL 28.5
4
T2 -1 = 17.5
1.75
NL+1=9.5
NL+2.5=11
9
1/4 DOS 6.2
front armhole line
center chest line
0,5
1/2
CW 25.5
M3
lapel fall
T3 -4
CF
1/2
3
2.5
4
3
1/2
1/2
18
Coat
single-breasted
front
3
2.5
4
T1 +1.5=75
1.5
3

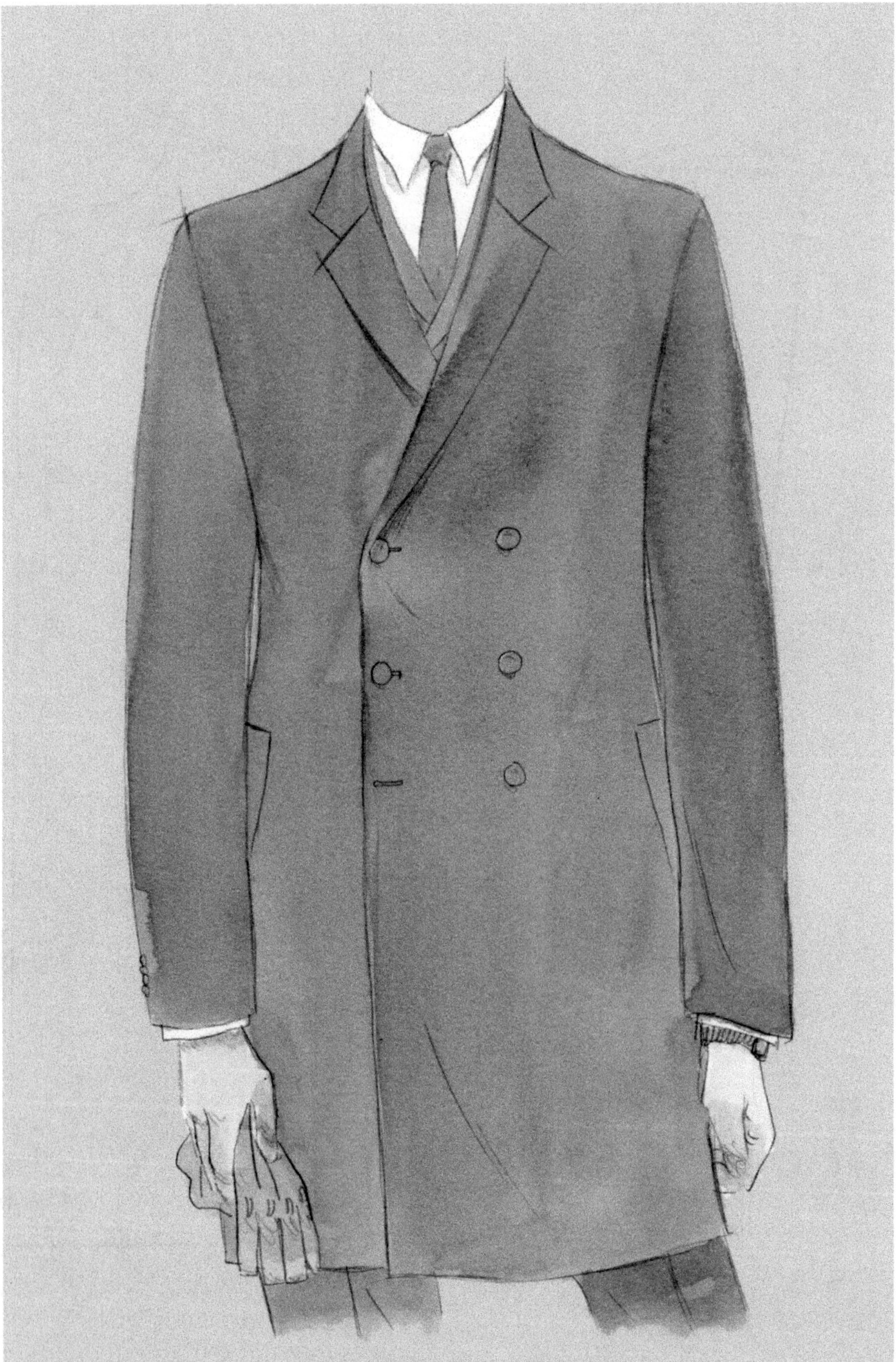

Manual for the double-breasted coat

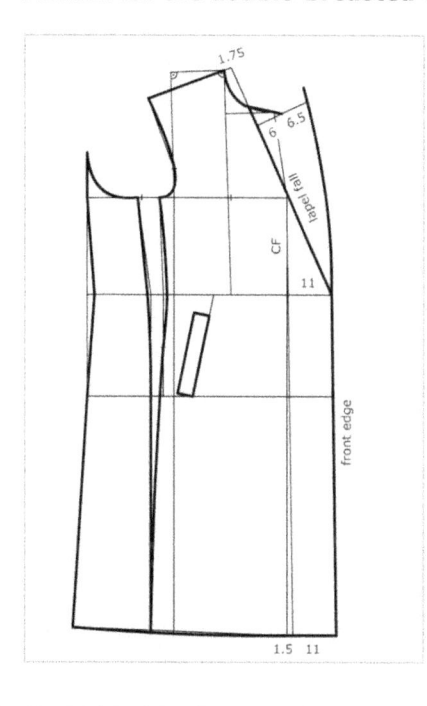

Neckline
- shape front neckline nicely

Lapel-fall
- extend shoulder-line to the right and mark 1.75 cm
- on chest-line from *CF*: square right and mark 11 cm
- connect both points
- n lapel-fall: square right to tip of *CF*/neckline
- on this line: first mark to the right 6 cm and then continue and mark 6.5 cm

Front edge
- on hem-line from *CF*: mark to the right 1.5 cm and connect with upper point
- on hem-line from new *CF*: draw to the right 11 cm and connect with upper point at front edge

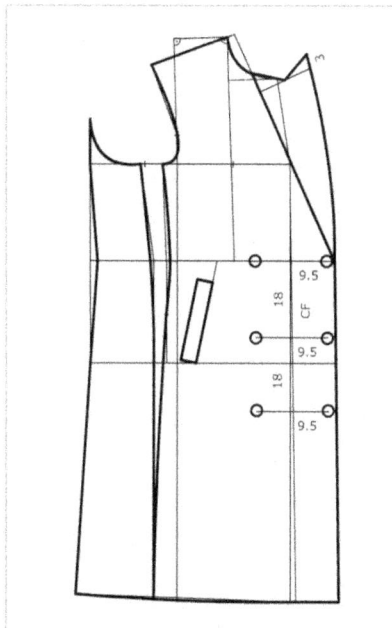

Lapel
- at lapel-edge: mark up 3 cm as shown
- finish lapel slightly curved as shown

Buttons
- on waist-line from *CF*: mark to each side 9.5 cm
- on *CF* from waist-line: mark down 18 cm
- mark the buttons at the same distances from the new front center as above
- continue with the lower buttons in the same way

Seam allowances when cutting

98

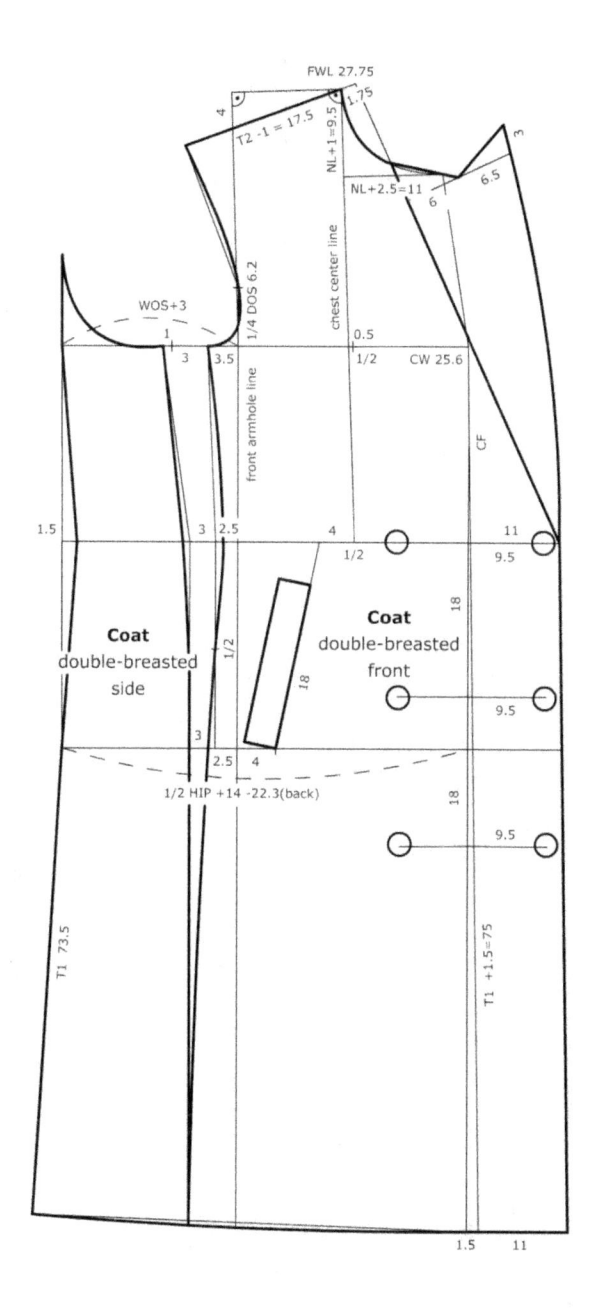

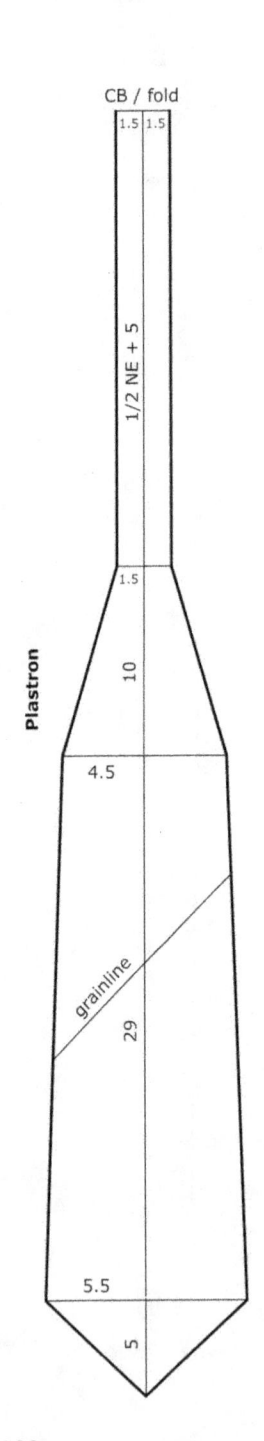

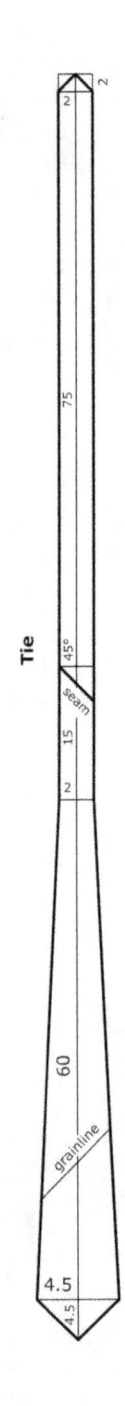

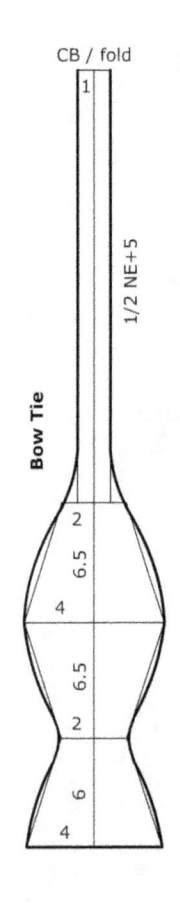

Plastron

CB / fold
1.5 | 1.5
1/2 NE + 5
1.5
10
4.5
grainline
29
5.5
5

Tie

2
75
45°
seam
15
2
60
grainline
4.5
4.5

Bow Tie

CB / fold
1
1/2 NE+5
2
6.5
4
6.5
2
6
4

Four-in-hand

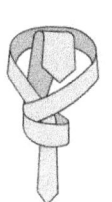

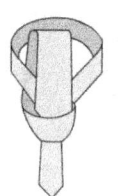

Half Windsor

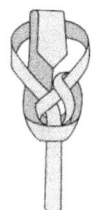

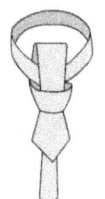

Windsor

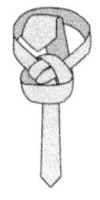

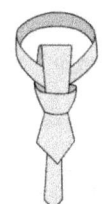

Bow-tie

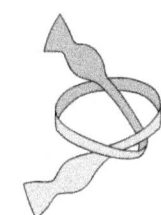

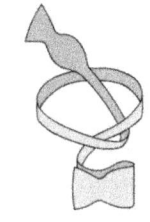

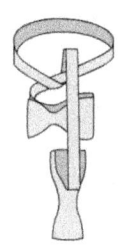

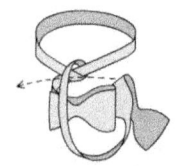

The right outfit for every occasion

Business wear
In general, the higher the position within the hierarchy, the darker the color of the suit should be. The same applies to festive occasions.
The classic business outfit consists of suit and tie. At high temperatures, particular attention should be paid to the quality of the fabric. In high-quality virgin wool no one comes up with a sweat.
With proper leg length of the suit trousers, the trouser hem ends about 0.5 to 1.0 cm above the upper part of the shoe heel. Socks should be long enough to cover the leg. In addition, a proper hairstyle and shave, as well as a good deodorant should be respected.

Smart casual wear
This is a casual business outfit. That means, the gentleman wears a day suit, but can omit the tie.

Casual wear
For example, the gentleman wears trousers with a jacket and a polo shirt. The tie can be omitted here. In Italy and France, the jacket is often omitted. Instead, the wearer casually hangs the sweater over his shoulders. The motto "No brown in town" is no longer valid here.
Accordingly, brown shoes or corduroy suits are allowed.

Casual friday
Although casual friday is an American invention, it has meanwhile also found its way into European companies and large corporations and is regarded as being in line with the approaching weekend. The gentleman wears jacket and trousers, here a clean, not tattered jeans is also possible. A tie is unnecessary. Linen suits that are less likely to be worn during the week due to their crumpling properties are now an option.

Dark suit
The dress code "dark suit" means a black suit with a plain-colored shirt (best in white) with double cuffs and cufflinks. These include absolutely elegant black shoes.

Cutaway

To a cutaway in black or gray, a vest should be worn in light gray or powder blue. "Stresemann" pants and a white shirt with double cuffs and cufflinks are mandatory. The cut is combined with a silk plastron in silver gray, a handkerchief in white and a cylinder in black or silver gray. The matching lace-up shoe here is a black classic "Oxford".

Tuxedo / Dinner jacket

The tuxedo is the slightly less formal, but still formal option to the tail coat. A tuxedo is black or midnight blue and is worn with a bow tie and vest or the so-called "cummerbund". The pants have a simple gallon on the side (satin stripes on the side seam).

Tail coat

The tail coat is generally worn only in the evening - after 18:00 - on very festive occasions. It is usually black or midnight blue and is paired with a white vest and a white bow tie. The gentleman wears black silk knee-socks and black patent leather shoes, preferably without lacing. The trousers should not be worn with a belt, so the pants do not have any belt loops, but they have a double gallon at the side seam.

Protection & care for your favorite pieces.

Your own washing machine is not the right place for bespoke clothes. The upper cloth, inner lining and lining would be exposed to extreme hardships and would certainly suffer. In addition, the colors fade.
In case of heavy soiling you prefer to bring your clothes to the dry cleaning - but not too often. Even the chemical agents put a lot of strain on the fabrics, once or twice a season should be enough.

With regular care you can achieve a lot. Air your clothes good after wearing. The textile fibers absorb moisture and remain elastic, and annoying nicotine or other odors disappear. You can also treat your clothes to a steam bath, which is especially good for trousers and skirts made of wool. Just hang them in the bathroom after showering. The wool fibers relax and wrinkles are smoothed out.

If you do not wear your favorite pieces, give the fibers recovery on the hanger. Brush your clothes in between with a soft natural hairbrush - e.g. horsehair - , to free them from the daily dust. Do not use synthetic bristles, they will damage the fabric. Similarly, adhesive rolls should be taboo, as adhesive residue can stick to the fabric fibers.

Small spots can be removed with a damp microfiber cloth. When heavily soiled, it is best to always bring the whole costume or the whole suit to the dry cleaning. Otherwise, different shades of color can be created, which harm the uniform appearance.

Garment bags protect your clothes from dust, mites and moths. They are also ideal for transporting your bespoke pieces. When you arrive at your destination, however, the wardrobe should be unpacked again so that it can air. If you want to store your things in a garment bag, you should make sure that it is breathable and made of natural fibers. So the fibers of your Garments can breathe and recover.

Natural moth protection. The wood of the American Red Cedar, which smells very pleasant to humans, is unbearable for moths. You can therefore keep your wardrobe moth-free with cedar wood pieces. Hang two to five cedar pieces freely in your closet so that they are not covered by clothing.

Laundry and care symbols

⊠	Do not wash	⊙	Tumble dry high heat
③⓪	Machine wash cold 30° C (80° F) synthetics cycle	○	Tumble dry low heat
🖐	Hand wash only	⊠	Do not tumble dry
④⓪	Machine wash warm 40° C (100° F)	□	Line dry (US only)
④⓪	Machine wash warm 40° C synthetics cycle	|||	Drip dry (US only)
⑥⓪	Machine wash hot 60° C (140° F)	−	Dry flat (US only)
④⓪	Gentle/wool wash cycle	⟋	Dry in the shadow (US only)
⊗	Dry clean only	⟋	Line dry in the shadow (US only)
⊗	Do not dry clean	⟋	Drip dry in the shadow (US only)
⌇	Iron high heat (max. 200° C)	⟋	Dry flat in the shadow (US only)
⌇	Iron medium heat (max. 150° C)	△	Bleach
⌇	Iron low heat (max. 110° C)	△	Non chlorine bleach
⌇	Do not iron	⊠	Do not bleach

Abbreviations

B
BPL   Back pants length
BW   Backwidth

C
CB   Center back
CF   Center front
CHE   Chest
COS   Circumference of scye
CVP   Cervical vertebra point
CW   Chest width
CW   Chest width

D
DOB   Depth of breast
DOH   Depth of hip
DOS   Depth of scye

F
FPL   Front pants length
FS   Front shoulder
FSH   Full shoulder
FWL   Front waist length

H
HEI   Height
HIP   Hip
HOS   Height of scye

I
INL   Inside leg

L
LG   Length

M
M   Measure

N
NE   Neck
NL   Neckline
NTK   Nape to knee

O
OUTL Outside leg

S
SH   Soulder width
SL   Sleeve length
SLH   Sleeve head
SLHW Sleeve hem width
SLW   Sleeve width

T
T   Transfer
TH   Thigh

U
UPA   Upper arm

W
WAI   Waistline
WB   Waistband
WL   Waistlength
WOC   Width of cuff
WOL   Width of leg
WOS   Width of scye

Michael Ross

Born in Munich.
After graduation, trained as a costume tailor at the *Bavarian State Opera*.
From 2007 studied fashion design at the *Kunsthochschule Berlin-Weissensee*.
This is followed by a one-year Erasmus stay in Brussels at the *École Supérieure des Arts Saint Luc, Bande Dessinée*, where Michael Ross met scenarist *Nicolas Wouters*.
The two worked together to create their first graphic novel titled *Lauter Leben*, which was published in print in 2013 in France and 2014 in Germany at *Avant* publisher's.

Their second book entitled *Totem* was also published in October 2016 by Avant. Michael Ross lives and works in his adopted home of Berlin.

www.mikaelross.com

Sven Jungclaus

completed his training as a bespoke lady's and men's tailor in the 1990s with *Heinz-Josef Radermacher* in Dusseldorf. Already at that time he worked for musical productions like *Grease* and *Forever Plaid* in Dusseldorf as well as *The Beauty and the Beast* and *The Fearless Vampire Killers* in Stuttgart.

After eight years at the *Bavarian State Opera* in Munich as a master tailor and head of men's costume, he has deepened his expertise at the *Royal Shakespeare Company* in Stratford upon Avon, the *Deutsche Oper am Rhein* in Dusseldorf and the *Salzburg Festival*.

Since 2013, he has been producing bespoke clothing for men and women in his tailor shop *Gewandmanufaktur* in Salzburg. In addition, the versatile tailor works again and again for the costume workshop *Das Gewand* in Dusseldorf and is requested for operas or musical productions - e.g., the *Metropolitan Opera* in New York, the *Nasjonale Opera* in Bergen, the *Theater Basel*, the Musical *Chicago* in Stuttgart and Berlin, *Het Muziektheater* in Amsterdam, the *Salzburg Festival* or the *Theater of Nations in Moscow*.

Another project of Sven Jungclaus is *Become-a-tailor*, an internet presence with professional tips on workmanship, patterns and instructions as well as other know-how for many costume epochs.

www.becomeatailor.com

Register

7th Cervical vertebra	10

B

Back vent	68
Back width	11
Back-pants	17
Back-pockets pants	21
Bow-tie	100
Breast circumference	9

C

Care symbols	105
Casual friday	102
Casual wear	102
Cervical vertebra point	25
Chest circumference	9
Chest width	28
Circumference of scye	80
Classic collar, shirt	52
Coat, single-breasted	85
Coat, double breasted	97
Collar single-breasted jacket	76
Collar double-breasted jacket	82
Collar stand	76
Collar width	9
Collar, shirt	76
Crease	16
Cuffs	47
Cutaway	103

D

Dart pants	20
vest	30
jacket	63
Depth of hip	57
Depth of scye	10
Dinner jacket	103
Double-breasted vest	35
Double-breasted jacket	79
Double-breasted coat	97

E

Elevated waist	57

F

Flap pockets	64
Fold pants	15
Front armhole line	28
Front edge, shirt	41
Vest	29
Jacket	62
Coat	90
Front pants	16
Front waist length	12
Fullness pants	18

H

Height	10
Height of scye	70
Hip circumference	9
Hip circumference	9
Hip-line	15
How to tie a bow-tie	101
How to tie a tie	101

I

Inseam pocket pants	17
Inside leg	13

J

Jacket collar, single-breasted	76
Double-breasted	82
Jacket sleeve	70
Jacket, single-breasted	57
Double-breasted	79

K

Knee-line	15

L

Lapel fall	62
Laundry symbols	105

N

Nape to front waist	12
Neckline	25
Norrow armhole at vest	27

O

Openeng vest	29
Outside leg	12

P

Pants	15
Piping pockets	17
Plastron	100
Pleat-line	15

S

Seat-seam	20
Shirt	39
Shirt collar, english cutaway	51
Shoulder basic line	25
Shoulder width	11
Side part seam	64
Side vents	68
Sleeve head shirt	46
Jacket	72
Sleeve length	12
Sleeve shirt	46
Jacket	70
Sleeve vent shirt	47
Jacket	74
Sleeve width	70
Sleevehead	70

T

Tailcoat	103
Taking measurements	8
Tie	100
Tilting side part, jacket	65
Coat	92
Tip of vest	29

Tuxedo	103
Tuxedo collar	50

U

Under sleeve	72
Upper arm width	70

V

vest narrow armhole	27
Vest, single-breasted	25
Double-breasted	35

W

Waist	57
Waist circumference	9
Waist length	10
Waistband	9
Washing instructions	105
Washing symbols	105
Welt pocket Vest	30
Jacket	64
Width of back pants	18
Width of cuff	47
Width of leg hem	16
Width of scye	60
Width of thigh	13
Windsor knot	101
Wing collar	50

Y

Yoke	40

Product informations:
Titel: Modern Ladies Tailoring, 256 pages
Author: Sven Jungclaus
Publisher: Books on Demand
ISBN: 9783750496156
Size: 15.5 x 1.6 x 22 cm
Available from autumn 2020